Interviewing and Interrogation

Interviewing and Interrogation

Second Edition

Don Rabon
Tanya Chapman

CAROLINA ACADEMIC PRESS
Durham, North Carolina

Library of Congress Cataloging-in-Publication Data

Rabon, Don.
  Interviewing and interrogation / Don Rabon, Tanya Chapman. -- 2nd ed.
     p. cm.
  Includes bibliographical references and index.
  ISBN 978-1-59460-195-8 (alk. paper)
  1. Interviewing in law enforcement--United States. 2. Police questioning--United States. I. Chapman, Tanya. II. Title.

  HV8073.3.R328 2009
  363.25'4--dc22

                                    2009024434

Carolina Academic Presss
700 Kent St.
Durham, NC 27701
Telephone (919) 489-7486
Fax (919) 493-5668
www.cap-press.com

Printed in the United States of America

To the people without whom this would not have been possible:
Don and Rachel; Bill and Nancy.

Contents

Preface

Like everything else, the scope of the interview process has changed drastically since the initial publication of *Interviewing and Interrogation*. At that time, when giving consideration as to who conducted interviews, foremost in the mind were investigators from local, state, federal, and public sector agencies. That is no longer the case. For example, now there are more private sector investigators than governmental. Additionally, with the passage of the Sarbanes-Oxley Act in 2002, auditors, who to that point occupied themselves primarily with the examination of the books and business practices, find themselves having to interview those who possibly may be "cooking the books" or involved in off-the-books fraudulent activities, and having to determine as to the veracity of the information the interviewee provides during the conduct of an audit.

Public sector interviewers who from time to time have a bad day in the interview arena generally do not suffer adversely with regard to continued employment. That is not the case in the private sector. A daily review of the headlines reveals circumstances wherein auditing firms are being sued for failing to detect fraud during the conduct of their auditing procedures. As a result, in some cases, firms fail and auditors suffer the loss of employment.

So now there are a multitude of professionals finding themselves tasked with having to conduct interviews in situations such that if the interview is conducted poorly, the downstream consequences are profound. Human resources professionals have to interview with regard to employment and during administrative investigations. Managers must interview subordinates with regard to personnel complaints and subsequent actions. School principals must interview students as well as teachers in situations ranging from skipping class to allegations of sexual impropriety between a teacher and a student.

As a result, the revision of this text is structured to apply to a vast array of interviewers regardless of what their job task responsibilities may be. After all, interviewing is interviewing, deception is deception, and persuasion is persuasion.

Suggestions on How to Best Use This Text

The text is presented in a manner designed to underscore the point that no element of the interview process—detecting deception, questioning, or persuasion—is an isolated event. All components are interrelated. Questioning is directly related to detecting deception and persuasion, and vice versa. Toward that end, even though there are specifically titled chapters, information regarding detecting deception is found in the chapter on questioning, information related to questioning will be found within the chapter on detecting deception, and so on down the line, including the appendixes. In this mode, action, effect, and rationale are, when necessary, presented together as a whole to enhance the learning association link and subsequently the effective application.

The information presentation provides application questions encouraging the reader to stop and consider the operation of the topic under examination to the interview process. These questions endeavor to link what the reader has learned from life's lessons outside the structured formal interview itself. The goal is to assist in applying what is already known from a lifetime of experiencing interpersonal communication dynamics and transferring that knowledge directly the conduct of the interview.

Additionally, there are points within the text wherein a comment is provided regarding the topic being presented. These are designed to place special emphasis on the importance of the subject matter at hand and to expand on its application. Ideally at these points, the reader should write his or her own set of application questions regarding the topic and its application, particularly to his or her own interviewing responsibilities or interviewing skill level aspirations.

Last, there are a number of exercises provided throughout the text. These three text design concepts—presenting information in an interrelated constellation format, application questions, and comments—are designed to allow those new to the interview process to establish a solid interviewing foundation, as well as to allow for more experienced interviewers to increase the borders of their interviewing options and effectiveness. For both, the reading and application of the material requires effort. Similarly, for both, the learning is in the effort.

We always enjoy hearing from those involved in the interview process and endeavoring to improve their capabilities. If you have a question, comment, or observation, our email addresses are dwrabon@msn.com and te.chapman@hotmail.com, respectively.

Introduction

Interview and Interrogation: What's the Difference?

The examination of the processes of inquiry and persuasion has to begin, for the interviewer, with the contrast between the interview and the interrogation. The term *interrogation* can have a very negative connotation for some. To those individuals, interrogation means bright lights, threats, force, and the "third degree." Whether writing an after-action report, summarizing an inquiry, or testifying in court, the guiding advice is to avoid the use of the term *interrogation*. In the corporate world, human resource personnel, legal counsel, and others all recoil at even the thought of the word. Even prosecutors would prefer the term be avoided in the articulation of a description of the communication event. With the negative connotation of this usage aside, it is important for the interviewer to understand what he or she is accomplishing within the conduct of the interview. Whatever is substituted for interrogation—be it persuade, convince, gain compliance, cajole, and so on—our examination will show the outcome is the same because it is not the use of the term that is the issue. You can have an excellent career as an interviewer and avoid the use of the term *interrogation* exclusively. The issue is the criteria of the interview process, which must be successfully accomplished on a regular basis and in an appropriate manner.

It is always interesting in a seminar involving experienced interviewers to identify the various criteria by which we separate these two modes.

Application Question 1:   How do we differentiate between an interview and an interrogation?

Answers from interviewers include:

Interview	Interrogation
Auditor's interview	Investigators interrogate
Involves a witness	Involves a suspect
Involves a victim	Involves custody
No Miranda rights	Requires Miranda rights

General information	Specific facts
Less demanding	More demanding
Casual	Highly structured
Interview in the field	Interrogate at the office
Information not known	Confirm known information
Scattershot approach	Pin-down approach

All of these are applicable considerations. Perhaps, however, the difference between the two can be articulated by framing the concept in terms of *the willingness of the interviewee* (i.e., the individual from whom you are to gain information or whose behavior you wish to influence). Imagine, regardless of where the interchange with the interviewee takes place—in the more commonly thought of interview room, in the interviewee's office, or in circumstances where the interviewee does not recognize the fact that you are formally interviewing them—the interviewee could, psychologically speaking, choose to sit in one of two chairs: the "willing" chair or the "unwilling" chair.

In the "willing" chair, the interviewee—whether target of an investigation, neutral third party, or an individual part of a routine audit—is ready to tell you whatever you need to know:

- what he or she did;
- what he or she saw or heard;
- what he or she knows

Consequently, all that is required here is the questioning technique appropriate to recovering the information from the interviewee. Simply stated, the interviewee is *willing to cooperate.*

On the other hand, the interviewee could choose to sit in the "unwilling" chair. Here, the interviewee is reluctant to provide the needed information or cooperate. Though we do not normally think of a victim as unwilling, a victim of fraud who is embarrassed to think about what has happened to him or her (much less talk to you concerning the ordeal) would fit this description. An adult male who has been taken advantage of financially due to his own greed or willingness to operate outside the law would be another example. Many witnesses or persons on the periphery of an inquiry are reluctant (unwilling) to become involved or participate in the interview process. Regardless of their individual roles, they share one area of commonality—they are unwilling.

The interviewer faced with a subject in the "willing" chair has only one task—to interview him or her   whereas the interviewer faced with a subject sitting in the "unwilling" chair has a two-step task: first and foremost, to move the interviewee from the "unwilling" chair to the "willing" chair, and second, interview him or her. Therefore, we can think of interrogation as the movement of the interviewee from the "unwilling" chair to the "willing" chair. It is as simple as that and as complicated as that—which is why we call it work. This task provides the challenge to the interviewing profession. Simply stated, as interviewers, we are responsible for changing behavior. Our objective, with regard to the individual in the "unwilling" chair, is to *change someone's mind.* That in itself is remarkable—to change someone's mind. Think about it for a moment.

If the interviewee is a target of an inquiry, then changing his mind could be detrimental to his own well-being, perhaps even drastically so. The information, evidence, or whatever we have in a particular circumstance may be weak or even nonexistent. Our only hope is to persuade the interviewee to change his mind—literally to get him to talk himself out of his own well-being. Theoretically speaking, if he remains in the "unwilling" chair, he still maintains the possibility to prevail or minimize the consequences. If he moves to the "willing" chair, he must face the consequences of his own actions. Thankfully, in a democratic society, we do not have the options of beating, threatening, depriving, or unduly influencing the subject. Our only option is to persuade, not compel.

In the interaction, the interviewer's approach should always be, "I am going to treat this person the way I would want to be treated if I were sitting in that chair." Our foundational prime directive is: we never—ever—want to do anything that would make an innocent person make an admission to something he has not done. We never want to take away the volitional component of the movement from the "unwilling" to the "willing" chair.

For the most part, as interviewers, all we have to work with are words, phrases, and sentences with which to change someone's mind. Certainly, the presentation of documentation, data, and information contrary to that which the interviewee asserts is important, but at the end of the day, how the interviewer treats the interviewee is the most critical factor.

What happens when we change a mind? Imagine, from a physiological perspective, the unwilling mind has a certain chemical composition and electrical configuration. What we attempt to do through the use of words can be compared to altering this composition or configuration. Put another way, the interviewee had a predetermined course of action in mind that now has changed to the very course of action we had in mind. Remarkable!

It is no wonder that in ancient times that words were thought of as possessing magical qualities. In a very real sense, they do. Words can be used to mend a relationship or comfort a distraught mind, and words can persuade. Words can create pain, anxiety, and all sorts of adverse circumstances. Interestingly enough, we all have access to the same words. For interviewers, the question becomes: What are we going to do with our words?

Application Question 2: Based on your experience and knowledge, how do you move the interviewee from the "unwilling" chair to the "willing" chair? How do you get people to cooperate?

Answers from interviewers include:

Ask general questions.	Make them feel this is what's best for them.
Win them over.	Gain their confidence.
Take away the foundation.	Relate to them.
Explain the facts.	Give them a way out.
Deescalate the crisis.	Give them a chance to explain.
Explain the advantages of cooperation.	Lie to them.
Downplay the disadvantages of cooperation.	Understand them.
Use deception.	Hang it on them.
Play on their sympathy.	Put it on them.
Play on their conscience.	Threaten them.
Determine their frame of mind.	Get them to trust.
Talk to them.	Mimic their manner.
Know how far to push.	Empathize.
Get on their level.	Imply things.
Speak their language.	Show them what they're looking at.
Show them.	Show them acceptance.
Tell them.	Develop rapport.

As we can see from these answers, various strategies are used by interviewers to influence the actions of the subject. Although there is a wide range of options, those listed here tend to share one characteristic—they are all generally stated. How do we "take away the foundation," "mimic their manner," "speak their language," "get on their level," or "make them feel this is what's best for them"? It has been the authors' experience that interviewers who say these things can, in fact, do these things. The difficulty experienced by interviewers is how to articulate or define *how, when,* and *why* to use these techniques. What we ultimately work for here are the specifics of defining the how, when, and why of moving someone from the "unwilling" to the "willing" chair.

Think of the relationship between interviewer and an unwilling interviewee in the following terms:

$$I \rightarrow S = B$$

where **I** represents the interviewer, who acts as the stimulus; **S** represents the subject (interviewee), who is the object of the stimulus; and **B** represents the behavior of the interviewee. The formula indicates the interviewer, acting on the subject, produces a behavior from the interviewee.

Recognizing that nothing happens in a vacuum (meaning the interviewer's verbal, vocal and nonverbal stimulus always elicits some behavior from the interviewee), the question for the interviewer becomes: Is my way of communicating with this individual going to produce the desired behavior? The interviewee will always present behavior—there is no way he or she can prevent him- or herself from doing so. But is the behavior demonstrated by the interviewee the behavior that we desire? If not, does the interviewer have the capability to modify his or her approach to one that will produce a more desirable behavior on the part of the interviewee? To state this simply: What can I do to move this individual from the "unwilling" to the "willing" chair?

How can it be some behavior is always produced from the interviewee? The individual cannot help but be affected by the interviewer. Perhaps you have noticed in the past, as you observed an individual during the conduct of an audit-related interview or a more formal inquiry, that he had assumed a certain posture. Then you noticed, as you proceeded with the conduct of the interview, he shifted his posture in the chair and made various other subtle yet observable positional changes in hands, arms, feet, and so on. Your transition of the interview from topic to topic had an effect on him. He changed. From the moment you enter the interviewee's environment, you begin to have an influence on him or her. What will be the end result of that influence?

There is a tendency on our part to give ourselves credit if the interviewee's behavior is what is wanted. However, if the interviewee's behavior is not what is wanted, we tend to blame the interviewee. For example, we could go into a group of interviewers and ask one of them a question such as the following: "That audit you were conducting that involved the chief financial officer taking kickbacks from vendors—how did that interview work out?" You could get an answer such as, "Oh, I interviewed that guy, all right. After a while, I had him eating out of my hand. I had him start crying and that was it. I got him to tell me everything."

Here we notice a rather lengthy answer, with all the pronouns and action verbs referring to or crediting the interviewer: "I interviewed," "I had him," "I got him." Continuing, we might ask, "What about that case of the bank clerk you knew was involved in fraudulent overrides—how did that interview go?" The answer might be, "I don't know what the guy's problem was; he had an attitude that wouldn't quit." Now we have a very brief response, with the blame for an obviously unproductive interview going to the interviewee.

These responses demonstrate human nature in action. If it went well, I did it; if not, then it was not my fault. The oldest example of this shifting of responsibility, you might recall, comes from the Old Testament. When God observes Adam in the Garden of Eden and sees that Adam, now recognizing his own nakedness, must have eaten the fruit of the Tree of Knowledge of Good and Evil, God asks, "Who was it that caused you to eat of the tree?" Adam replies, "It was the woman, the one you gave me, that caused me to eat"—an interesting and all-too-human reply. Supposedly, there were only two people living there—Adam and Eve. Yet when Adam replied, he qualified his answer. He did not simply say, "It was the woman," but added, "the one you gave me," implying it was both God's fault and Eve's fault. (Eve, of course, blamed the snake.) In all probability, however, they would each have taken a bite sooner or later. It was just a matter of whom the persuader got to first.

Although shifting the blame can be an excellent compliance-gaining technique, it is very irresponsible for the interviewer to shift blame for the outcome of the interview onto the interviewee. If we are going to take credit when the interviewee's behavior is what we want, then we have to take responsibility when the interviewee's behavior is not what we want.

We can't have it both ways—all credit and no responsibility. To say it is not one's fault when things do not go well means that when they do go well, it was just dumb luck. In both cases, we are the interviewer, the one responsible for making things happen. No matter how the interviewee behaved, for the most part, we did something to cause him or her to behave that way. If what we do does not producing the desired behavior, do we have the capability to transition to an approach that will produce a more desirable behavior?

Having laid the foundation of interviewing precepts, let us begin.

Interviewing and Interrogation

Chapter 1

A Template, a Set of Requisite Skills, and a Process

The interview process, like any discipline, has a set of specific criteria that apply to operate effectively. The interviewer must know *what* must be accomplished—the template; *how* to do it—the requisite skills; and *when* to do it—the process.

Consequently, interviewing requires the combination of a series of high-level cognitions. The interviewer who knows what to do but not how to do it is not going to be consistently successful. Along the same line, the interviewer who knows what to do and how to do it, yet lacks the knowledge of the when, will also meet with unsatisfactory results more often than not.

For example, an individual may know that an open question has specific functionality. That level of knowledge is only informational. However, the person may not know how to ask an open question—the knowledge level. Should the interviewer know what and how, without the third level—judgment—knowing when to ask an open question, the first two levels are of little use.

In the following, we examine each of these three elements individually and subsequently combine them into one operational unit. Together they provide the foundation for maneuvering the interview to its successful conclusion.

The Interviewing Template

A template is defined as "anything that determines or serves as a pattern; a model" (Dictionary.com). The pattern or model of the interview is as follows:

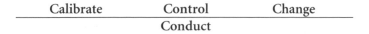

Calibrate	Control	Change
	Conduct	

With regard to this interviewing template, "conduct" can be verbal, involving words, vocal (silence or sounds), and nonverbal (body language on the part of the interviewee). Our examination of the interviewing model begins with calibration.

Calibrate

The interview involves knowing when the interviewee is truthful and when he or she is deceptive to the point of articulation. The interviewer has to be able to articulate to him- or herself as well as others the basis for such an evaluation. It will not suffice to conduct an interview and make the determination, "I have a feeling that the individual is deceptive." It may be the interviewer's feeling is absolutely correct—the individual *is* deceptive—but having a feeling is not enough to justify an adverse administrative action, obtain a warrant, or arbitrarily focus an investigation on one person exclusive of others who may be suspect. The truth of the matter, in this circumstance, is no one is interested in the interviewer's feelings. They want to know particulars— when the interviewee was truthful and when the interviewee was deceptive. They want to know the substantiations for the evaluation.

In all probability, the interviewee was both truthful and deceptive! As an example, in a given circumstance, within the interview, there may be four salient points that need to be covered—topics A, B, C, and D. In this case, the interview involves the exploration of the development (A), advertisement (B), awarding (C), and evaluation (D) of a contract to an outside vendor. In three of the areas (A, B, and D), the interviewee has elected to be truthful. Only in topic area C—the awarding of the contract to a vendor even though it was not the lowest bid—has the interviewee elected to deceive. Topics A, B, and D are true. Only topic C is deceptive. The interviewer cannot summarize the interviewee as simply truthful or deceptive. In fact, the interviewee is both, only at different points within the interview. The interviewer must separate the wheat from the chaff—the truth from the deception—and have the ability to articulate a rationale for the delineation of the two. Even if the interview does not result in an admission, at the very least the interviewer knows the topic area—C—requires further investigation and inquiry during the postinterview activities.

In a similar manner, the focus of the interview could be an individual's activities on a given day, events concerning a missing deposit bag, or facts relating to the disappearance of a child. In any case, the emphasis herein is the ability to calibrate the interviewee's conduct.

Calibration involves the interviewer acutely observing (more about this later) the conduct (verbal [words], vocal [sounds], nonverbal [observable behavior]) of the interviewee when he or she is presenting what is known to be true. It is the same concept as a patient with a doctor. The patient "presents"—displays or articulates certain symptoms. It may be at one level of physical activity (A, B, and D) the patient presents in a certain manner, but at a higher level of physical activity (C), the patient presents a different set of symptoms, allowing the doctor to note the deviation from the baseline, make an evaluation, and move forward accordingly with the patient.

Within the interview, attend to the interviewee's "presenting" conduct when he or she is providing information known to be true. This calibration of baseline conduct can be established when addressing ancillary topic areas, such as work history with the organization, duties and responsibilities, educational history, family, and so on. As the interviewer transitions into the elements of the interview, he or she now has a baseline to identify changes in the interviewee's presenting conduct. Ideally, he or she will be able to note the deviations from the interviewee's baseline conduct, identify the deviations, apply the appropriate labels, and ultimately return to those points within the interview wherein the deviations occurred with amplification questions.

Control

Our second element of the model involves control. Within the interview process, control is the ability to induce a reaction. The reaction again, may be verbal, vocal, or nonverbal. The goal of the interviewer is to both produce and evaluate the reactions of the interviewee guiding the interview process to its predetermined goal.

Consistently effective interviewers endeavor to have a level of control that enables us to have "the ability to perform," rather than limiting our effectiveness in dealing with others by only having "control over." An interviewer functions on one of the following four levels of control.

Paycheck Control

Paycheck control comes with having a job—a position. The position could be a sworn law enforcement officer, a proprietary investigator, an auditor, and so on. This kind of control involves having some level of direct or indirect control over someone. Therefore, in reality, the control is not in and of itself *within the interviewer*, it is within the organizational entity that *hired the interviewer*. Stated simply, the control the interviewer has is vested in a job someone gave him or her, and someone could, in turn, take it away. Paycheck control is the lowest level of control for two reasons.

1. It is not an individual skill set taken on by the interviewer.
2. It is minimally effective if the interviewee has no regard for the authority attached to the paycheck the interviewer receives.

The majority of times an interviewer has lost control of an interview, it is because he or she depended on paycheck control to win the day, and when that did not suffice, he or she having no other abilities to employ, became frustrated and then angry, thus losing control of him- or herself and subsequently the interview.

Participant Alliance Control

Interviewing participant alliance control (PAC) is the ability to convey to the interviewee that the interviewer fully intends to treat the individual in the manner he or she would want to be treated if sitting in the other chair. PAC is more of a mindset than a skill level. It is as much a reflection of how much personal control the interviewer has over him- or herself as it is how much control the interviewer has over the process. It has a direct bearing in the performance level and ultimate success of the interviewer. It is vital the interviewer understand his or her mission is not to judge the individual but to gain information and compliance from the interviewee. Interviewers do not wear black robes. People do not stand up when the interviewer walks into the room. They are not referred to as "the honorable" anything. Their undertaking is to know all, not to judge. The attitude conveyed by the interviewer is one of endeavoring to understand and comprehend.

The interviewer must keep in mind whatever it is the interviewee may (and *may* is the operative word here) have done, he or she did not do it personally to the interviewer. If he or she possibly stole organizational assets, these assets did not belong personally to the interviewer. If he or she killed someone, it was not the interviewer who was killed. At the point wherein the interviewer begins to personalize rather than objectify the interview process, PAC has been lost. Once it is lost, it most difficult to reestablish.

Capability Control

Capability control is having the capacity to know and perform. Interviewers who have capability control operate at a level that involves personally incorporated skills. They are successful within the interview because they use appropriate communication techniques with the interviewee, rather than attempting to exercise control over the interviewee. Capability control is not something someone can give to the interviewer. Consequently, it is not something someone can take away, like a badge or a position.

Capability control is an ability level the interviewer has taken on for him- or herself through individual study, training, and experience, fueled by a desire to be the very best at the interview process. Wherever the interviewer with capability control goes, the skill level goes with him or her. It is not an external, job-dependent function. It is an internal skill level.

Effecting Control

Effecting is defined as "production of a desired impression" (Dictionary. com). Effecting control enables the interviewer to produce the desired impression on the interviewee to obtain the desired outcome—compliance. The interviewer with this skill level is consistently successful.

This individual knows, within the shifting environment of the interview process, what to do as well as how and when to do it. For the interviewer endeavoring to attain this level of control, the journey is challenging and continuous. Each interview is a learning experience. He or she continually evaluates and strives to improve on abilities and talents. This individual is deeply involved in the human dynamic of the interview process. He or she reads, trains, retrains, and interacts with like minded interviewers to learn from the experiences and observations of others.

Admittedly, the levels of control beyond the first (get and keep a job) to the fourth require effort on the part of the interviewer. To advance beyond the lowest level requires time and energy. Human nature being what it is, each interviewer advances to the level for which he or she is willing to expend the time and effort. Like a pyramid, the largest percentage of interviewers are found within the paycheck control level, followed by participant alliance control, capability control, and last, with the smallest percentage of interviewers found in the tip, effecting control.

Change

Without a doubt, the only constant within the interview process is change. When the interview involves two participants—the interviewer and the interviewee—there are three variables, all by definition subject to change. Those three variables are:

- the interviewer,
- the interviewee, and
- the issue on the table.

It is incumbent on the interviewer to control the change. Like the helmsman on a ship, making the subtle changes on the rudder to adjust to current, wind, and location, the interviewer is always aware of his or her position and the planned destination of the interview journey and is capable of making the appropriate adjustments to stay on course. Let's look back at our example.

During the conduct of the interview, the interviewer employed the following strategy—a nondirective interview using open questions supplemented by secondary questions. As the interviewer is addressing topic areas A, B, and D the conduct of the interviewee (verbal, vocal, nonverbal) is displayed by his willingness to respond fully with regard to the elements of each topic. However, as soon as the interviewer addresses topic area C—the awarding of the contract to a vendor even though it was not the lowest bid—the conduct of the interviewee drops (changes) to below the level conducive to effective interviewing. Now, if the only approach the interviewer has is a nondirective interview, then the interviewing "vessel" is dead in the water. This delineated approach will work well with topic areas A, B, and D but will not suffice for topic area C.

The interviewer must be able to adjust (change to) the shift that has just occurred in the interviewing current. This requires the interviewer first to change what he or she is doing to an appropriate technique that will transition the interviewee's conduct from subpar back to a level conducive to going forward. Therefore, a change in the conduct of the interviewee is precipitated by an initial change in the interviewer—capability control.

For illustration, we compare the process to a fishing trip. In this instance, the fisherman goes out early in the morning with only one lure. The lure travels along the top of the water. Initially the sun is low on the horizon, and the fish are feeding near the top of the water. The fisherman is catching fish readily. But as the sun rises in the sky, the water warms up, and the fish go down to a deeper, cooler level. Because the fisherman only has one lure and it remains on the surface of the water while the fish are now at another level, the fishing day is over. If, however, the fisherman has a whole tackle box of lures—plugs, spoons, rubber worms, and so on—which he knows how to use, he can continue to fish successfully all day. It is a matter of knowing how to adjust to the movement of the fish and conduct the fishing strategy accordingly.

Likewise, the interviewer maintaining a tacklebox of interviewing techniques can change accordingly and continue to succeed where other interviewers might come up short. It is a matter of knowing what technique (lure, if you will) to employ that will allow the interviewer to identify what caused the interviewee's conduct to deteriorate—"go down" with regard to topic area C. Having identified the cause, the interviewer addresses the reason in a manner designed to remove the barrier to productive interviewee conduct. In this manner, ultimately topic area C will be just as fruitful as topic areas A, B, and D.

A Set of Requisite Skills

As with any critical endeavor, the interviewing dynamic requires a set of requisite skills necessary to function in a quality manner. The required skills are the ability to:

- elicit a response,
- detect deception, and
- gain compliance.

Addressed simply to the interviewer, one asks the following:

- Can you cause someone to talk to you on a consistent basis?
- Once the individual begins to talk, can you determine when they are truthful and when they deviate from the truth?
- If there *is* deception, can you change the deceiver into a truth teller?

The criticality of these skills is such that an entire chapter is allocated for each of them.

A Process

A process is defined as "a continuous action, operation, or series of changes taking place in a definite manner" (Dictionary.com). Ideally, an interview is a continuous action. By having a process, the interviewer should always know his or her location on the interview path, be oriented as to where he or she is going, and have the capability to identify and ultimately remove any barriers hindering the progress and ultimate success of the interview. The interview process can be outlined as A, B, C, and D.

A: Allow the interviewee to speak. Questions are the working tools for the interviewer.
B: Be attentive to the interviewee. Although this element of the process on the surface would seem to go without saying, in reality, paying attention is an element of the process that is neglected with resulting adverse outcomes. Paying attention requires effort and discipline. The individual is unable (or even unwilling) to achieve a high performance level with regard to element B will never come close to functioning when faced with the requirements of element C.
C: Center on changes in conduct. These changes in interviewee conduct—verbal, vocal, and nonverbal—may be overt or subtle. Nevertheless, it is critical to note the changes in light of the point within the conduct of

the interview at which the changes occurred. At this point within the interview, it is not to be inferred just because there are changes in conduct that they are automatically in and of themselves the result of deception. Any number of emotive or environmental factors (heat, cold, etc.) can result in a verbal, vocal, or nonverbal change. It is enough at this point to simply be aware that the change occurred to utilize element D.

D: Direct the subsequent, amplifying questions into the areas at which a conduct change was noted.

The A-B-C-D interview flow process necessitates the interviewer ask questions that allow the interviewee to talk; attend acutely to the interviewee as he or she talks, note changes in verbal, vocal, and nonverbal conduct; and ultimately place interview-expanding questions in the areas wherein the changes were noted. In this manner, the interviewer is oriented, knows his or her position on the interview path, and moves incrementally toward the ultimate destination—to know the truth.

Summary

At this point the interviewer:

- is equipped with the understanding of the role of the template to the conduct of the interview;
- is aware of the three requisite skills necessary for success; and
- is knowledgeable of the four-step, A-B-C-D interview process.

As we continue, we explore in depth the components delineated to this point. We move from a macro overview to a micro examination—transition from a magnifying glass to a microscope. After all, isn't it true that "the devil is in the details?"

Chapter 2

The Honest Truth about Detecting Deception

And oftentimes, to win us to our harm,
The instruments of darkness tell us truths,
Win us with honest trifles, to betray's
In deepest consequence.

—Macbeth

Rick: *"I'm always thinking, what kind of answer can I give this man without giving him nothing. Regardless of the question that has just been asked, I am thinking what kind of answer can I give him so that he can go on and I can go on."*

As we noted in Chapter 1, it is incumbent on the interviewer to determine the veracity of information provided by and the deportment of the interviewee. This determination must be more than just a feeling. It may very well be that the feeling of the interviewer with regard to the interviewee's veracity is most accurate. However, the interviewer must be able to articulate—to him- or herself and others—what was seen and heard during the conduct of the interview that formed the evaluation and the resulting actions on the part of the interviewer.

To study deception is to study the history of humankind. The noun *deception* is derived from the Latin verb *decipere*, which means "to deceive." People have always sought to deceive or ensnare one another for their own purposes.

The various types and techniques of deception, as well as the motives for attempting to deceive, have been in evidence since recorded history. The Old Testament prophet Isaiah, for example, believed one could discern others' wrongdoing in their facial expressions: "The shew of their countenance doth witness against them." Francis Bacon (1561–1626) seemed to agree when he noted, "a man's face gives his tongue leave to speak," adding, "for the discovery of a man by the lines and expressions of his countenance is a great weakness and betraying." Charles Dickens also believed it was possible to identify deception in the face of another. His classic novel *Great Expectations* contains a scene with two convicts whose stories are conflicting accounts. "'He lies!' said my convict, with fierce energy. 'He's a liar born, and he'll die a liar. Look at his face; ain't it written there? Let him turn those eyes of his on me. I defy him to do it.'"

As stated, the interviewer has the necessary task of determining whether an interviewee is deceptive, identifying the nature of that deception, and changing falsehoods into truth during the interview process.

Deception can be an uncomfortable topic for some interviewers to address. They have a tendency to take deception on the part of the interviewee as a personal affront. This is an interviewing foundational key. If interviewers do not grasp this element, they are forever doomed to be an ineffective, frustrated, mediocre interviewer. Remember this: If the interviewee is deceptive, he or she is not acting against you personally. *Never* personalize the interview process. Always keep the objective in mind. If the individual stole something, he or she did not steal it from you. If he or she shot someone, it wasn't you. Whatever the person did, it was not done to you. If it was done to you, you should not be conducting the interview. Along those same lines, if the interviewee is resorting to deception, do not react the way you would react if someone you cared about was deceiving you. The interviewee is not your child, spouse, friend, or loved one. You are being paid to conduct the interview. It is a job, a profession requiring no small level of professionalism and skill. Do not marginalize yourself by becoming personally involved in the interview process. Once you do, effectiveness is no longer in play. It is generally true in life that when we are the victims of overt lying, we respond more angrily and take it more personally than when information is withheld from us—concealment. This is not your personal life, this is a professional undertaking.

The following response, by a male interviewer from Kentucky, was offered in reply to the question, "What tends to make you mad?": "A liar. It makes you think that they think that they are smarter than you. I don't like some of these people you come in contact with thinking that they are smarter than I am." Similarly, a female interviewer from North Carolina responded to the same question as follows (S = Subject Interviewed, I = Interviewer):

S: A liar. I hate a liar.

I: Why?

S: Usually because I can see through it because I lie sometimes. And I can usually see through a liar. And it infuriates me when I can't break them.

I: Can you give us an incident of the last time that you lied?

S: The last time that I lied? I can't think of one right off the top
of my head.

Both interviewers indicated being lied to by the interviewee resulted in
anger—a loss of self-control. The second interviewer also revealed while she
could accept her own lying to others, being lied to made her angry. She expressed what is true of all of us.

Responding to the falsification of others with personal outrage is a typical
human reaction. As Proverbs 13:5 reminds us, "A righteous man hateth lying."
However universal such a response may be, as interviewers we need to modify that response in our professional responsibilities. As our examination will
show, if an interviewee is going to attempt to deceive us, we want him or her
to do so by means of falsification. Our attitude is, if he must deceive, then let
him lie!

Hopefully our examination will underscore this fact and if necessary establish a mindset that evaluates deception on the part of the interviewee as an
asset to the interviewer and not a source of angst.

Although deception has always been in evidence, indicators say the willingness to deceive is increasing dramatically and the tendency to feel badly
about having deceived is decreasing proportionally. So get used to it! Deception has always been here, and it is not going away. If you are going to react
emotionally every time you run into it in the course of your interviewing responsibilities, you will find yourself being tired a lot.

Deception Defined

We can define *deception* as "action or speech designed to mislead another"
(*Penguin Dictionary of Psychology*). A simple definition has been selected to
examine a complicated process. The concept of action is the initial focus of
our study of deception. First let's tighten up the definition just a bit and sub-
stitute "conduct" for "action." Now we can break down the foundational components of deception on the part of the interviewee as follows:

- Conduct is verbal, vocal, nonverbal (words, sounds, and body language);
- Cognition (thinking) precedes conduct;
- Conduct is directed toward the achievement of a goal—in this case, to
  mislead another.

From the foregoing, we can see that deception is a conscious operation on
the part of the interviewee. No one deceives by mistake; it is deliberate con-

duct. It is the deceiver's goal, his or her objective. All this conduct involves is directed toward attainment of the objective—to deceive the interviewer.

Look for Changes in Behavior

If the goal of the interviewee is be truthful (topics A, B, and D from Chapter 1), his conduct—verbal (V), vocal (VO), and nonverbal (NV)—is directed toward that end. We illustrate this here.

Goal
Interviewee behavioral conduct—verbal (V1), vocal (VO1), nonverbal NV1)--->
Truth: A, B, D.

If the goal of the interviewee is to deceive (topic C), his or her conduct will deviate (change) in some manner from the behaviors necessary to be truthful. The change can be overt or subtle.

Goal
Interviewee behavioral conduct—verbal (V2), vocal (VO2), nonverbal (NV2)--->
Deception: C.

Therefore, the interviewer endeavors to note when the interviewee's behavioral conduct changes, and subsequently at the appropriate point within the interview, places additional questions into the areas in which the conduct changes were noted.

Goal
Interviewee behavioral conduct—(V1), (VO1),(NV1)---> **Truth:** A, B, D.
Interviewee behavioral conduct—(V2), (VO2), (NV2)---> **Deception:** C.
Question Question Question

Concealment (Secrecy): The Easiest Form of Deception

Deception is used to hide or conceal (see, e.g., Proverbs 10:18). If the interviewee has elected to deceive, his or her first option—the first club out of the bag—is most often going to be deception via concealment. Concealment is easy because it is passive. To deceive by concealment, all the interviewee has to do is nothing—just leave it out. For example, the salient points of the interview are topics A, B, C, and D. Topic C is the element that poses a psychological threat to the interviewee. Consequently, to deceive by concealment he only has to respond with, "A, B, __, D." The deceiver does not have to overtly do anything with regard to deception via concealment. He or she only has to leave the (in his mind) problematic component out. For example:

> On Monday the employee went into work at eight in the morning (A).
>
> He worked on the development of a new software program for which his employer was under contract (B).
>
> He downloaded proprietary information (which he planned to sell to his employer's competitor) to a jump drive which he placed in his pocket (C).
>
> He left work at four in the afternoon (D).

He is asked,   "What happened Monday, from the time you got to work until the time that you left?"

He replied,   "I arrived at work at eight in the morning (A). I worked on developing the new software program which is my current assignment (B). I left work at four in the afternoon (D). A, B, __ D.

Many experienced interviewers succumb to deception via concealment. It is subtle. It comes in under the radar because it is not so much about what *is* there as much as about what *is not* there. It underscores the importance of paying attention to the behavior of the interviewee at all times. There are indicators of deception via concealment (addressed later), but to note them the interviewer has to totally be in the moment with regard to the conduct of the interview.

Detecting the possibility of deception by concealment is only the prelude to all that has to be played out within the interview from this point forward. The interviewer's mindset must be such that he or she is thinking, "Even if there is deception by concealment, the possibility exists that the deception has nothing to do with what is important to me." There is a very real possibility the concealment is not relevant to the purpose of the interview. The interviewer must place appropriate questioning techniques into the areas in which the indicators of the possibility of deception via concealment and endeavor to cause the interviewee to reveal what has purposely been left out of the narrative. Only then can the interviewer determine the relevance of what has now been made known. For example, once, one of the authors was interviewing a young man who was under suspicion of having committed a murder. As the young man articulated his activities during the day in question, there were three distinct points within his narrative wherein the indicators of deception via concealment were presenting. After a break, questioning was focused into these three areas with the goal of having the interviewee reveal what had been concealed. In the fullness of time, the young man shared that on the day of the murder, he and his girlfriend—who was not the deceased—had argued in the morning, again that afternoon, and in the evening he had slapped her in the face. He had purposely taken those details out of his narrative. Concealment is concealment. Consequently, the symptoms of deception via concealment presented even though they had nothing to do with the issue at hand. Only by identifying the symptoms and subsequently questioning through the concurrent narrative areas was the truth brought to light, the suspicion removed from the young man, and the investigation continued to a successful conclusion.

Falsification-Simulation: The More Difficult Form of Deception

Once the interviewer has identified and eliminated the haven of concealment (we will address how in Chapter 3) desired by the interviewee, it will become necessary for the interviewee to ultimately resort to the other major form of deception—falsification. Falsification occurs when people attempt to portray themselves or something else—facts, actions, circumstances, and so on—as something they are not. An example of falsification would be the linguistic behavior of Jeffrey MacDonald (Appendix B), whose conviction indicated he attempted to portray himself as a victim of the same attackers who killed his wife and two daughters. He attempted to misrepresent his actions of that night to the interviewers during the interview.

With falsification, unlike the passive omission of concealment, the interviewee is forced to act and, of necessity, lie. This form of deception-simulation occurs, according to Francis Bacon, when an interviewee "industriously and expressly feigns and pretends to be that which he is not." Herein we see the difference of this form of deception. We now have an interviewee simulating or overtly acting the role of someone he is not, a type of affirmative deception. Again, MacDonald can serve as an example of a falsifying interviewee, for his conviction indicated he attempted to feign (simulate) one set of facts regarding the night in question when in reality it was another set of facts altogether.

It is not at all unusual for an interviewee to resort to both forms in an attempt to successfully deceive. The interviewee can variously choose to conceal or distort the truth. Awareness of the two forms can enable the interviewer to determine the purpose of the interviewee's attempt to deceive: Does the interviewee wish to present something that is not true, or does he or she wish to hide from the interviewer what really is true?

In his own consideration of these two types of deception, Bacon observed, falsification was the more reprehensible form of deception than closeness, reservation, and secrecy. He qualified that judgment, however, when he added, "except in great or rare moments." (Oddly enough, Bacon also maintained there are times when deception, even in its most culpable form, is justified. Certainly it would seem so to the deceptive interviewee who has much to lose if caught in a deception.)

Why? As Bacon noted about the first form of deception, it offers very little to observe or be taken into consideration. But once the interviewee (maneuvered to do so by the skilled interviewer) finds it necessary to engage in the other deception form—falsification—he or she is now forced to act, to do something to deceive. The interviewer has moved the interviewee from a state of inactivity to one of activity—and activity can be observed and evaluated more readily.

For the interviewee who can effectively deceive by means of falsification, the advantages include:

- causing the unskilled interviewer to lower his or her defenses and thus gaining the advantage;
- gaining or regaining the initiative of the interview;
- determining what's in the mind of the interviewer.

Disadvantages of the use of falsification on the part of the interviewee include:

- revealing one's fearfulness;
- destroying the impression of accuracy;
- becoming obvious to others;
- replacing the interviewer's belief in the interviewee with disbelief.

Indicators of Concealment and Falsification

Just as a physician will evaluate a patient's symptoms to diagnose an illness, an interviewer evaluates an interviewee's "symptoms" for signs of the possibility of deception. The physician does not react to those symptoms; rather, they are used to assist in formulating a diagnosis. This diagnostic process should be exactly what the interviewer undertakes as well. The interviewer should use whatever symptoms of deception he or she observes as the interviewee presents, not react angrily to them.

As always, when the interviewer is evaluating an interviewee and the possible use of deception by that interviewee, the key word is *change*. The key is how the interviewee changes behaviorally in relation with him- or herself. There is no behavioral change, subtle or overt, that can be labeled with all certainty as occurring as a result of deception. Noting change is not the end, it is a means to an end. Any number of emotive or environment factors can result in behavioral changes on the part of the interviewee, separate and apart from deception.

As a general rule, most interviewees display some emotionally reactive response in conjunction with deception, especially by falsification. (As Proverbs 6:13 describes such behavior, "He winketh with his eyes, he speaketh with his feet, he teacheth with his fingers.") At this stage, all the interviewer can say with certainty is that the behavior changed. He or she cannot assert that it changed because of deception. Once behavior change is noted, at an appropriate point within the interview the interviewer will return to the issue at hand when the change occurred with additional probing questions to note how the interviewee presents with the increased focus on the related topic.

The question is, "When does the interviewer return to those points wherein change was noted with the additional questioning?" The operative number is *three*. Do not be in a hurry to immediately address an issue in play at the point where a change of behavior was noted. Let the interview continue to flow, with the interviewee thinking all he or she is asserting is being readily accepted. At the point the interviewer begins to probe, the interviewee will transition to a more heightened state of awareness, and the "shields" will begin to go up. At the point the probing begins, the effect on the downstream consequences of the flow of the interviewer is a certainty. Wait until you have a minimum of three issues to probe before you transition from listening to probing.

For example, the skilled interviewer will:

- watch for a change in the rate of eye blinking;
- note changes in movement of the interviewee's feet and legs; and
- attend to changes in movement (increase or decrease) of the interviewee's hands and fingers.

The interviewee's attempts to deceive will normally result in increased anxiety and stress. The stress must be released from the body. The release of the stress will be physically expressed—by the interviewee's body through what are commonly known as *adaptors*.

The stronger the rapport (Appendix A) between interviewee and interviewer, the greater the stress experienced by the interviewee once he or she elects to use deception. The greater the stress experienced by the interviewee, the more obvious the bodily stress release indicators—adaptors—become to the interviewer. However, keep in mind a highly complex falsification can result in diminished adaptors. As always, the only reliable criteria is how the interviewee's conduct changed in relation to him- or herself.

There are many unexpected benefits derived from the interviewer's investment of time and effort in establishing rapport with an interviewee. See Appendix A for more.

Interviewee's Physical Symptoms as Stress Relief

As Francis Bacon advised those who would endeavor to detect the physical signs of deception, "Wait upon him with whom you speak with your eye, for there be many wise men that have secret hearts and transparent countenances." The interviewer should look for the following behavior changes:

1. Dryness of mouth
2. Restlessness
   A. Changes in position concurrent with a topic change or in conjunction while responding to a question
   B. Tapping feet
   C. Fidgeting
   D. Gripping arms of the chair
   E. Elbows held close to the body
   F. Running hands through the hair
   G. Chewing of fingernails, pencils, or other objects
3. Excessive sweating
4. Pulsation of the carotid artery
5. Pallor, flushing, or change in complexion
6. Excessive swallowing
7. Avoiding direct gaze
8. Appearance of being disturbed and/or very tense
9. Audible turbulence in the stomach

Remember, these physical manifestations of change may or may not indicate the presence of deception. One should not base any such conclusion on the observation of one indicator. The interviewer should watch for clusters of symptoms, noting where these occur in the interview. Use the noted changes to guide you with regard to your subsequent questioning and enable you to articulate to yourself and others what you saw and heard that guided your questioning.

Belief in the Interviewee

The interviewer should begin from a position of unconditional belief in the interviewee; it should require some effort by the interviewee to make the interviewer change his or her mind or modify his or her original position. It is okay to have a theory, but do not be so attached to it you block out any information—verbal, vocal, nonverbal—that runs counter to the theory. Entering the interview situation with a set-in-stone predetermined belief that the subject is guilty and/or deceptive is counterproductive to the process of inquiry and persuasion and is likely to influence the interviewee's responses adversely.

Even the innocent will feel and exhibit some degree of nervousness in an interview setting. The interviewer should strive to reduce the interviewee's level of anxiety. If the interviewee's anxiety is only attached to the interview itself, simply getting him or her to talk will reduce this anxiety in a short period of time. This person is simply anxious about being interviewed. He or she is not the doer of the wrongful deed. However, the individual who is anxious because discovery of wrongdoing has a distinct possibility of not relaxing as readily as the innocent. This anxiety is attached to a greater danger, not the interview in and of itself. Accordingly, the interviewer should look for any behavioral changes beyond those baseline readings displayed by the subject as the interview began.

As we already noted, the effort to deceive results in stress, and that stress will be physically manifested. In an interview, Rick expressed an insight of profound importance to the interviewer: "When you tell the truth and you're getting the same punishment. And that's what it is." To tell the truth and not be believed, he states, is a form of punishment. For the truthful individual, the consequences of telling the truth and not being believed are the same as those experienced by the guilty. As Rick puts it: "And that's what it is." The end result is the same, according to him: "And he gives you the same punishment as if you did it." Stress can also be the result of telling the truth and not being believed. That stress will also be physically manifested and may signal a change.

The interviewer who, inadvertently or deliberately, conveys disbelief to the subject will be likely to observe stress-related symptoms, but in this context the interviewer will be unable to determine whether the physical manifestations of stress are (a) deception-generated internally by the deceptive subject, or (b) interviewer-generated externally by disbelief in the truthful interviewee. The interviewer who has an automatic tendency to disbelieve every interviewee, requiring "proof" of each one's truthfulness, should remember what Seneca wrote about 2,000 years ago: "It goes far toward making a man faithful to let him understand that you think him so; and he that does suspect, I will deceive him, gives me a sort of right to do it." This observation supports the necessity of the interviewer's presentation of believing the interviewee so whatever physical signs of stress that may be observed can be assumed to have been internally generated, and not as a result of stress imposed externally by the interviewer.

This limitation also applies to certain direct approaches that begin with an accusation at the beginning stages of the interview. The interviewer cannot rely on the interviewee's physical responses to such an approach because a deceptive individual will react because of his or her own attempts to deceive, and the innocent will react because of the interviewer's disbelief, which is a necessary feature of the direct approach. Paradoxically, once the interviewer is ready to confront the interviewee with disbelief, the physical signs of stress should no longer be an issue. That moment in the MacDonald interview (Appendix B), for example, is illustrated by the interviewer saying, "Your story doesn't ring true. There's too many discrepancies. For instance, take a look at that picture over there." At this point, the interviewer would no longer need to use physical reactions in evaluating the subject. However, the interviewee's verbal responses would continue to be useful indicators of the possibility of deception.

Interviewee's Verbal Responses as Deception Indicators

Francis Bacon again makes an excellent point regarding the evaluation of honesty or deception in the words of others, advising us to "consider their ends" and to "interpret their speeches." The interviewer should listen for the presence of any of the following dynamics in the interviewee's responses:

1. Attempts to evade questions
2. Vague answers
3. Conflicting information
4. Different answers to the same or similar questions
5. Falsehoods or inaccurate information

6. Inability to commit to their own narrative through the use of terms such as "normally, usually, sort of, kind of, basically," etc. (The use of these terms provides the interviewer with excellent probing points to explore the possibility of deception via concealment.)

A falsehood stated by an interviewee can provide the interviewer with much more than just a deception indicator. Because of the interviewee's inevitable difficulty with remembering deceptive assertions made earlier, it becomes increasingly possible he or she will inadvertently reveal the truth. As Proverbs 12:13 reminds us, the deceiver can be caught by his own words: "The wicked man is snared by the transgression of his lips." It is interesting to note *deception*, which has the root meaning of "to ensnare," can be in turn the snare of those who practice it. This ensnaring of the "wicked" by their own words gives a significant advantage to the interviewer.

Often this inadvertent revelation of the truth occurs in one word or as an aside, where the interviewee comments on his or her own narrative. This serves once again to underscore the importance of every word uttered by the interviewee: Each is worthy of the interviewer's attention and consideration. For example, consider the use of the word *say* in the following excerpt from MacDonald's narrative. What in particular does the use of "say" in his aside reveal?

"So, in effect, I was blunting everything by, you know, holding this up. And I couldn't get my hands free—out of this thing. And I remember I ended up, when I was laying on the floor—I forgot to say that— when I woke up on—it was still all around my hands and everything, and I took it off as I was going in the bedroom. And after I took this knife out of my wife's chest, I—you know, as, keeping her warm. You know, to treat shock, elevate the legs and keep them warm."

Another interviewee inadvertently revealed the truth during a homicide investigation interview. The interviewee, who claimed he hadn't killed the victim himself but saw what had happened in a vision, responded to questioning as follows.

I: Okay. Let's go back to what you talked to me about yesterday.
S: Okay. I was in my daddy's house about 4:30. And then suddenly I was over at … I saw somebody go in over at my neighbor's house. And they opened the door and it was a man. And uh … the door wasn't locked. She was waiting for her lover to come home or something.
I: Now stay on the right track.

S: That's what I'm trying to do. And the man came in there …

I: What did she have on?

S: She had black panties on. And she had a bra on. A black bra. A black bra or a bathing suit. But it was black. So this guy comes in. Didn't say nothing. Now I know.

I: What did you tell me yesterday?

S: But my visions are more clearer today.

I: Tell me what you told me yesterday. What did he say?

S: I was too high on my medicine. I was talking out of my head.

I: Yeah. But what did he say?

S: Uh … He said, "How you doing?" And then uh … she laid there on the couch. Across the couch. She had a rope across the couch. I know that. Or something like that, it was a decoration. It was a white couch. And then the man said uh … do you know who I am and all this stuff or something like that. And uh … the man attacked the woman. She was on the couch and she jumped up and he pushed her. Then she hit the couch and fell on her back. So at this time he runs over in the kitchen and gets a knife, a steak knife, a great big chopping knife. And comes back. And by this time the lamp was knocked over. And she picks up something with her right hand and that's how I got cut right here on my knuckle.

Perhaps we now understand MacDonald's successful falsification depended on specific lines he had to "say." From the second interview, we know the interviewee did not get cut on his knuckle during a vision. If the interviewer can attend to the interviewee effectively, he or she may hear the truth being inadvertently revealed more often than would be expected. The following list includes several types of deception indicators for which the interviewer should listen.

1. Excessive assertions of truthfulness.
   A. "I hope to die if I am lying."
   B. "Swearing on my mother's grave."
2. Evasive answers.
   A. "I am not sure what happened."
   B. "I don't think it could have been that much."
3. Broken or incomplete sentences.
4. Stuttering or stammering.

Exercise 1: The following transcript will illustrate some of the elements we have addressed above. In this pre-employment interview, would the subject be likely to engage in:

- concealment; or
- falsification?

Comment 1

I: Have you ever taken one of these before?

S: There were questions in there that were just unbelievable.

Here we note that the interviewee did not answer the initial question at all, commenting instead on the scope of some of the questions in the pre-employment questionnaire. The interviewer would make a mental note of this equivocation. The subject did not answer the question. Rick advised us with regard to his own use of equivocation: "To hell with the question that had just been asked. Go off into something else. Make a statement to something else." As an interviewer, make sure you know whether the interviewee answered your question. Do not drop into the trap of equivocation. Remember, any time you ask a closed question, it opens the door to the possibility for equivocation to occur.

I: Well, the first thing I'll do is to go over the questions that will be on there.

S: Okay.

I: That way, if you have a few questions, I'll be able to answer them for you.

S: Okay.

I: Before I do that, the first thing I need to determine is that you are not under a doctor's care for anything that might affect the test, are you?

S: No, sir.

I: Now, your on-the-job accident. You were off work for about ten days.

S: Approximately, yeah. I worked ... I was doing three different jobs at once. I was a carpenter. And the framing man had set up on a table and was sawing. He was using a C-clamp to hold a big piece of lumber. And I went over, and it was just about to cut through, and was standing there waiting for him to finish. And when he cut through it, it fell right down and fell on my left arm. I didn't know it until the inside of my jacket started to feel hot and I could tell it was bleeding.

Comment 2

Now the element of change comes into consideration. In the initial portion of the interviewee's last response, some modification occurs: "approximately." Also, we note the broken sentence: "I worked … I was doing three different jobs at once." Last, the interviewee used many more words and sentences to make a response than were strictly necessary. While the interviewer is not ready to make a judgment on the symptoms he has observed this early in the interview, he is nevertheless aware of change

> I: Now, this insurance company. Is it _____?
> S: Yeah. _____. It is my brother's business health insurance. He is in the business of home construction.
> I: And what type of work did you do?
> S: I did, well, I … worked for him. Let's see. Three different times, I guess … And he did framing, like for houses and garages.

Comment 3

Again, the interviewee provides an interesting response. We note the use of *well*—a word that allows time for pausing and reflecting. An instance of stammering occurs: "I … I worked for him." Next there is the sentence "Let's see." ("Let's see," which is a contraction of "let us see," is also found in the following question and answer sequence. Make your own determination of what is occurring at these points.)

We are also aware the interviewee did not answer one of the questions: "And what type of work did you do?" Instead, he responded with the number of times he had worked for his brother and the type of work his brother did. Remember to pay attention to pronouns. The pronoun *he*, as used here, indicates a great deal.

> I: Did you do that?
> S: Yeah. And also I dug foundations.
> I: And, all together, about how long did you work for your brother?
> S: Let's see, this last time I went there July, August, September, and October. So that was four months. And probably each time I worked for him was about four months. Probably about a year altogether.

[**Note 1:** The double use of the term *probably* serves to weaken the interviewee's assertion.]

I: And you put down here that you were a "self-employed contractor." What did that involve?

S: Yeah. I had, uh ... that was just a two-day job building some steps for a guy's trailer.

[**Note 2:** Observe the broken sentence, hesitation, and the use of the term *just*, all in a single response.]

I: Now what about _____?

S: Now, I started working there, must have been about three years ago.

[**Note 3:** The interviewee uses the term *must*.]

I: And approximately how long did you work there?

S: Until December of that year. And then I had, uh ... gone in for surgery on my left arm.

[**Note 4:** The interviewee hesitates over the statement: "And then I had, uh ... gone in for".]

I: Okay. And diesel mechanic, how long did you do that?

S: Okay. Let's see. I went to school for that in July, two years ago. And about a month later I spent some time with a friend of mine who is a diesel mechanic. I never actually worked for any company, but I just went out with him. Just to get some time under my belt. So I could go out and say that I had done roadside diesel repairs.

[**Note 5:** The interviewee offers an extended answer, with modification and the use of the word *say*.]

I: And with _____, what kind of work did you do?

S: I was a carpenter and a carpenter's helper.

I: And why did you leave the job with _____?

S: Okay. That ... I was laid off, uh ... about the middle of the year. I was laid off. See, I filed a suit. Because I had had surgery and _____ wouldn't pay for it. So anyhow, I had to go back home. And my brother told me that things were really slow there. So I was laid off. And then when I came back I was still laid off, and then I left.

[**Note 6:** The interviewee's response includes broken sentences, hesitation, and an extended answer.]

I: And then _____ why did you leave there?

S: I'm still employed by them. I'm just laid off.

I: And the work in diesel repairs, why did you stop doing that?

S: That I just couldn't do that with my arm. That was too much.

I: Okay. This is a question for a failure of a lot of people.

S: I didn't understand, so I didn't know what to put down.

I: Don't try to read things into these questions. Number one, I'm not a law enforcement officer. I couldn't care less what you say on this question but it explains that the important thing to them is, they just want you to be truthful. Now, on these drugs we have on this list here, all I need to know is, if you have tried it, when was the last time. And I just need a ballpark figure, days, weeks, months, whatever.

S: Oh, God, I don't know.

I: Well, like I said, just put it in the ballpark. About when is the last time you used speed?

S: I can't do that. I have ulcers. Any kind of ...

Comment 4

This is a revealing answer, to say the least. The question concerned time and implied the interviewee had used speed. In response, the interviewee does not deny the use of speed, but rather indicates why he cannot use it now: He has ulcers. Instead of responding to the effect he wouldn't or hadn't used speed, the interviewee replies he can't use it because of some restriction imposed on him.

I: Have you ever tried it?

S: Oh yeah, let's see. Must have been about the tenth grade.

[**Note 7:** Again, the interviewee uses the term *must*.]

I: That far back?

S: Yeah, it has been a long time. The only kind of drugs like that ... I've had downers as far as for ... I can show you my arm. See my arm. I've had stuff for that. The doctor was giving me synthetic morphine and I've had some hard-core drugs for my arm. But ...

I: What about actual illegal drugs?

S: Uh ...

[**Note 8:** The interviewee's total response is a sound: "uh."]

I: Were you using prescription drugs that were not prescribed to you?

S: Oh, I suppose. Gee, I don't know. Maybe a year ago.

[**Note 9:** The interviewee's response includes a number of equivocators: "suppose," "I don't know," and "maybe."]

I: And what about heroin?

S: No. I've never had heroin before.

I: What about LSD (acid) or mescaline or any type of hallu-
      cinogen?

S: Oh, gee ... Gee, let's see, probably ...

[**Note 10:** The interviewee responds with a broken sentence that
          includes "probably."]

I: What about cocaine?

S: No, I don't do that because of my stomach. I've got ulcers
      real bad. Anything like that I start bleeding real bad. You'd
      know right away.

Comment 5

This answer is most revealing in terms of the use of *because*. The interviewee responds with a reason that he does not use cocaine: Not because it is illegal or dangerous, but because it makes his stomach ulcers bleed. Given this
reason for not using cocaine, what would the interviewee be likely to do if the
negative effects of cocaine use were eliminated? Additionally, the interviewee
reveals his belief that if he did use cocaine, he would be discovered: "You'd
know right away."

I: What about angel dust?

S: No.

I: Anything else we don't have listed here?

S: No sir, that's about it.

[**Note 11:** The interviewee's last response implies something has
          been withheld: "that's about it."]

I: Okay. On the question of selling illegal drugs. Again all I
      want to know is that if so, about what the approximate value
      would be and what kind of illegal drugs it was. Now think.
      We're going back three years. So think about that for a
      minute.

S: Within three years? Uh ... I don't know. I haven't really sold
      a lot of drugs except for marijuana. Uh ...

Comment 6

Here is an excellent answer for evaluation. The interviewee begins his response with a question: "Within three years?" Next comes the hesitation: "Uh ..."
Then the interviewee's assertion is weakened by a preceding statement: "I don't
know." The terms *really* and *except* also provide the interviewer with material to

evaluate. The use of the word *except* reveals that the interviewee has sold a lot of marijuana. As for the other types of drugs, he hasn't "really sold" a great deal. Finally, the interviewee hesitates over the end of his response, with "uh."

I: Give me something you feel comfortable with ... $20,000?

S: Ha, ha, ha. No ... no. I ... I ... God, I don't know. Let's try ... uh ... $2,000?

[**Note 12:** What elements are to be found in the interviewee's entire answer?]

I: $2,000 sounds pretty good.

S: Somewheres. I don't know. I'm not a heavy drug dealer.

Comment 7

The statement "I'm not a heavy drug dealer" is an example of an inadvertent revelation of the truth. The interviewee's use of the present-tense verb *am* (in the contraction *I'm*) indicates the interviewee is a drug dealer now, an implication supported by the interviewee adding the modifier *heavy* to describe the extent of his drug dealing. Had the interviewee responded to the question by stating, "I wasn't a heavy drug dealer," or, "When I sold drugs, I didn't sell a lot," the evaluation would be altogether different. Remember, as we emphasized before, to pay attention to verb tenses.

I: And that was just marijuana?

S: Yeah.

I: It wasn't any heroin?

S: No, sir.

I: And you've indicated here you've never been in any trouble with the police at all.

S: No. Not since I was a juvenile ... like ...

I: I'm not worried about juvenile. Unless it was for something like murder ...

S.   No. No. Well, I went one time and uh ... I robbed a hardware store. But I went and said I did it, you know. I told them I did it. I went with my father over, and talked to the people.

[**Note 13:** What do you gather from this response?]

I: Well, on the $20 in merchandise taken from places where you've worked. What kind of merchandise was that? Just petty supplies?

S: I suppose, like, maybe some candy in a box or something like that, you know.

[**Note 14:** What do you gather from this response?]
I: Can you remember taking any money?
S: No, sir. I've ... I've ...
[**Note 15:** What do you gather from this response?]
I: You've probably never even worked near money.
S: Not in the past few years. Not since I was quite a bit younger.
I: Okay. You spent four months in the naval reserve?
S: Yes, sir.
I: Why did you get out?
S: Why? I had uh ... okay, I had ... I had pneumonia. I was out about a week. Then I had to go home for a funeral, so that was about two weeks. They wanted to recycle me. And after that I said, that was a breach of my contract. I couldn't help I got sick, I couldn't help about the death in my family.

Comment 8

Much is revealed in this response. What can you learn from the indicators present here?

Exercise 2: This exercise is based on the transcript of an interview from a missing person case. It is possible the missing woman is dead. Keep in mind the dynamics that have been covered in this chapter.
I: State your full name for me.
S: Bobby _____.
I: And your address, Mr. _____.
S: My address is _____.
I: All right. In May of _____, were you married to Donna _____?
S: Yes, sir.
I: All right, tell me about your marriage to this lady.
S: Well, from the time that we were, uh from the time that we were married in, in North Carolina, we had, uh, uh, no problems whatsoever until this, this deal turned up that you're asking about.
[**Application Question 1:** What does the interviewee's describing the relationship in terms of "no problems whatsoever" indicate? What inference can we draw from the broken phrasing of "this, this"?]
I: All right. Now you had two children by Donna before you were married?

S: Before we were married. Yes, sir.

I: And you started dating her when she was sixteen?

S: Uh, somewhere in that neighborhood. I don't remember exactly.

[**Application Question 2:** What does the hesitation sound "uh" indicate? What is significant about the statement "I don't remember exactly"?]

I: And you were how old?

S: I was somewhere in my twenties.

I: And you were still married to your first wife when you started dating her?

S: At the time being, yes.

I: All right. So you were basically running around on your first wife?

S: Uh, well, in a way we were, yeah, but we were separated. We were separated from each other, and, and uh, she uh, we had put in for a divorce.

[**Application Question 3:** What three elements do we detect in this response?]

I: Okay. And you had caught your wife having an adulterous relationship with someone, hadn't you?

S: Yes, sir.

I: All right. Have you ever caught Donna having an adulterous relationship with anyone?

S: No, sir.

I: Did you know that she was dating someone else at the time of her disappearance?

S: Uh, no, sir.

[**Application Question 4:** What do we note in this last response?]

I: You did not know that she was dating someone else?

S: Not until after, after she'd disappeared. You know, I didn't know that she was dating someone there. No, sir.

[**Application Question 5:** What does the presence of "you know" at this point and at others in the interview indicate?]

I: Well, when did you find out that she was dating someone else?

S: Whenever she disappeared, uh, people began to tell me the things about, uh, uh, about David and about him a' coming to the plant, and uh, standing there talking to her.

[**Application Question 6:** What do we detect in this response?]

I: Okay. Do you remember what people told you this?

S: Uh, I don't remember their names, but it was two girls that said that they worked on the same machine with her in the plant.

[**Application Question 7:** What two elements do we note in this response?]

I: Okay. How did you locate David?

S: Uh, through the girls.

[**Application Question 8:** What do we find an example of in this response?]

I: Well, did you have ...

S: Them, them girls, them girls told me that he, uh, that he, uh, worked for company and that's the way I located him, through the company.

[**Application Question 9:** What two elements are demonstrated by this response?]

I: It was the _____ company or _____ company.

S: Uh, well, uh, I'se been thinking it was the _____ company, but anyhow, he delivered to the machine there. It was the fountain-type drinks, and they said that she stood and talked to him, uh, till, uh, the boss man would have to go tell her to go back to work.

[**Application Question 10:** What is noteworthy in this response?]

I: Okay.

S: That's what they stated to me.

I: All right. So you didn't know about the relationship of your wife with David until after her disappearance?

S: That's right.

I: That's what you're telling me?

S: That's right.

I: All right. And these girls told you that?

S: Yes, yes, sir, they did. Yes, sir.

I: Did at any point you hire a private interviewer to locate your wife?

S: Afterwards, yeah, after, uh, after I'd done got the kids back.

[**Application Question 11:** What is noteworthy about this last response?]

I: All right. Was this in, within days or weeks of her disappearance?

S: In days. Yeah.

I: All right. How did you find out where your children were?

S: Uh, the lady called, uh, uh, the oldest girl, uh, the girl which is Mary, uh, Mary had told her that her daddy worked at a machine shop and that lady told me that she started calling all the machine shops in town, and she told the lady did, that the third call was whenever she got hold of me.

[**Application Question 12:** In addition to the other indicators that we have noted, what do we now recognize?]

I: Where were you employed at this time?

S: I was employed at, uh, a place called _____, there in town.

I: All right. At the time that your wife disappeared, did you have any reason to believe why she'd left you?

S: No, sir.

I: All right. Do you remember what day she left you?

S: No, sir.

I: All right. What are the circumstances of her leaving you?

S: Uh, that I really don't know. The, the only circumstance that, that I know of her leaving me was, was what I told you a while ago. That was, she stayed at home, said she was sick, and was going to, uh, uh, said if she didn't feel better, she was going to go to the doctor that day. And she said, and I'd a'been taking the kids up to school.

[**Application Question 13:** What three comments would you make about this response?]

I: Uh-huh.

S: And uh, uh, uh, she said instead of me a'taking 'em up there, you know, for her to go to work, that just leave 'em there with her, she was sick, she'd keep 'em herself. That's the day she left.

[**Application Question 14:** What is happening in the answer above?]

I: And you found out from the lady that owned the house from, across from you?

S: Yes, sir.

I: That, that you were renting your, your residence.

S: That's right.

I: On Smith Road.

S: And she's the one that does, stated to me that they left, a taxi picked her up around ten o'clock that day.

[**Application Question 15:** What can we learn from the interviewee stating "a taxi picked her up"?]

I: All right. She told you that they left in a taxi?

S: Left in a taxi.

I: What did you think when they left?

S: I had no idea. I had no idea. I didn't know, I didn't know
      they's gone until I came home that evening from work, at
      five-thirty was whenever I found out they's gone. When I
      came home, uh, at five-thirty that evening, my son, Jim, had
      come home from school, and he said they were not there
      whenever he came. So I went over to ask Ms. _____ if
      she knew anything about it, was the first that I knew. That's
      whenever she stated to me that, that she left with a taxi with
      two suitcases. Well, whenever she stated that she left with
      two suitcases, you know, I wondered why in the world did
      she do that.

[Application Question 16:   What is the most obvious indicator in the re-
                    sponse above?]

I: You didn't have any idea?
S: Had no idea.
I: Why she left you?
S: Why she left, had no idea why she left and took two suitcases
      because she stated to me she was sick and she was going to
      the doctor.
I: Did you ever find out where your wife moved to?
S: Where she went to?

[Application Question 17:   What happened in the response above?]

I: Yeah. Where she moved to.
S: Uh, not until after, uh, after, uh, whenever I told you that
      this detective found where she moved to. And uh, we went
      over there with that law that you're talking about there, that
      deputy or whatever he was.

[Application Question 18:   What three indicators do we find in this re-
                    sponse?]

I: All right. You went over there with a police officer?
S: Went over there with a police officer.
I: And what did you find when you got there?
S: Whenever we found over there, we found that the door of
      the house was standing open and that, uh, everything in the
      house was, was tore down, and the bed was turned down
      and there was blood in the bed.

[Application Question 19:   How would you summarize what you can learn
                    from the response above?]

I: Did anybody ever explain to you what the blood was?

S: The police officer stated to me that the blood was, uh, from a menstrual cycle.

I: A menstrual cycle.

S: Yeah.

I: When you describe the house as torn down, what do you mean by that?

S: Well, there wasn't nothing straightened up, you know, you know how a house would be early in the morning, you know, all the bed clothes is turned this away and, and uh, some of the kids' clothes was laying in the, uh, in the bathroom, in the floor, and uh ...

I: It wasn't neat?

S: It wasn't neat. That's right.

I: Do you believe that's where your wife was living?

S: Yes, I do.

I: Had you ever seen her at that apartment?

S: No, sir.

I: Had you ever seen her in the company of David, the man from the _____ company?

S: You talking about, well, the, what I stated there a while ago, when I seen that car, red car, pull off down at the, uh, uh, there's a café there.

[Application Question 20: What does the response above reveal?]

I: The Corner Cafe?

S: Yeah, when they, when they pulled up from, from down there, one evening whenever ...

I: You seen a photograph of David today?

S: Yeah.

I: Did you identify that man as the man that drove off with your wife?

S: No, sir.

I: From [the] Corner Cafe?

S: No, sir.

I: You've identified that man as the man that was in court?

S: Yeah.

I: When you were having a custody situation?

S: Yeah. Yes, sir. Yes.

I: But you'd never seen him prior to your wife's disappearance?

S: Uh, nothing except in, uh, like I said, whenever, uh, he pulled off down there, and I can't, I can't identify him exactly.

[Application Question 21: What does the phrase "like I said" indicate to us?]

I: Do you know where your wife is now?

S: No, sir.

I: You got any ideas?

S: No sir. Have no idea.

I: Do you know who your wife is with?

S: When?

I: When she ran off. Do you know who she ran off with?

S: The only thing that I know is what other people told me, and other people told me. I don't know. I can't say that she run off with David 'cause I never did see him and her except that one time that I thought was him, was the only time.

[Application Question 22: How would you summarize what can be gathered from the response above?]

I: Driving a red Toyota, four-door.

S: Driving a red car. I don't remember whether it was a Toyota or what. It was a red car.

I: Why did she leave that night?

S: I have no idea about it.

I: What'd she tell you when she got in that red car?

S: She didn't, she didn't tell me nothing.

I: When she came back, what'd you ask her about it?

S: Whenever she, whenever she came back, she said she'd went back to the plant to, to see about something or another that, uh, that she'd left down there or something.

[Application Question 23: What do we note in this response?]

I: How long was she gone?

S: Uh, not more than thirty minutes.

I: Long enough to …

S: Just, just long enough, long enough to drive, according to the way he stated to me, long enough to drive to the plant and back too.

I: You didn't question her about it?

S: That's, that's all I asked her about it. She said she left something at the plant and, uh, somebody took her back to get the plant. I don't recall even who she said took her back, but somebody from there at [the] Corner Cafe, she said. Somebody that, from there took her back to plant to get something she left down there, and she wasn't gone more than thirty minutes till she come back home.

[Application Question 24: What three aspects of this response do we note?]

I: Mr. _____, did you ever talk to your wife about getting a divorce?

S: No, sir.

I: Did you ever talk to your wife about going to a lawyer's office and getting separation papers?

S: No, sir.

I: Do you know how your wife got enough money to move into her apartment?

S: No, sir.

I: Did you ever pick up your wife where she worked?

S: Uh, uh, one time that I recall of, in the evening that we was taking the kids to the, gonna take the kids to see a doctor.

[Application Question 25: What three aspects of the response above do we note?]

I: Did you ever take your wife to work in the morning on your way to work?

S: No, sir. We worked different times.

I: What hours did you work?

S: Uh, she went to work earlier than I did. She went to work an hour earlier than I did.

I: And you never took her to work?

S: And I, I, I took the kids, whenever she left, uh, uh, going to work, I took her down to [the] Corner Cafe, uh, and I'd let her out and I'd take the kids to school.

[Application Question 26: How would you summarize what can be gathered from the response above?]

I: All right. Who picked her up at [the] Corner Cafe and took her to work?

S: She said it was some of the people that she worked with. I ...

[Application Question 27: How did the interviewee avoid answering the question?]

I: Did she ever identify anybody?

S: No, sir. She did not. Did not. I, I took it to be some of the girls she worked with, was what, uh, I took it to be.

I: What kind of car did you own?

S: Uh, Chevrolet.

I: What color was it?

S: Brown.

I: Was it two-tone, cream and brown?

S: No, sir, solid color.

I: Solid color.

S: Yes, sir.

I: And this is the same car that you saw in the photographs?

S: I owned a, a, before I owned it, I owned a, a, Chevrolet that was a two-tone.

I: Dark and light?

S: Uh-huh.

I: That was the ...

S: Yes, sir.

I: The newest car?

S: This was the newest.

I: Mr. _____, did you kill your wife?

S: No, sir, did not.

I: Do you have any idea where her ...

S: Did ...

[**Application Question 28:** What does the interviewee's attempt to ask a question at this point signify?]

I: ... body's buried?

S: No, sir. Do not. Do not.

I: Do you have any idea where she is?

S: No, sir. No idea.

I: Why haven't you supported Jane and Mary since ...

S: I supported Jane and Mary when my sister kept 'em, when they was little, to my sister.

I: Why didn't you support them after then?

S: Well, after that, they left town. Uh, Mary got married and Jane been married three or four different times.

I: How did you support them?

S: I give my sister money to, to take care of 'em.

I: How much?

S: If I'm not mistaken, I give her, I believe I give her $80 a month. That's what I give her.

I: Did you know they were not in town?

S: Yes, sir.

I: Where were they?

S: They was down in school in the county.

I: Did you pay for that?

S: Uh, no, sir.

I: Did you ever give your children credit, uh, Christmas cards?

S: Yes, sir.

I: You did give your children ...

S: Yes.

I: Christmas cards.

S: Yes.

I: Did you ever send your children Christmas presents?

S: Yes, sir.

I: You did?

S: Do. Still do.

I: You still send your children ...

S: Still do.

I: Christmas presents?

S: Still do.

I: When's the last time you saw your son?

S: I've not saw him in a, in a pretty good while. Uh, uh, he come over in, in, the area and, uh, the best that I could find out, he brung a bunch of dope over and made a big mess out of the, uh, out of, uh, the other children, uh, there at the trailer park. And uh, Ms. _____, that owns the house that they live in will verify that if you wanted to ask about that.

I: What about Mary? When was the last time you saw her?

S: I saw Mary, uh, I believe she was over here Christmas.

I: Did you talk to her about your wife?

S: No, sir. Did not.

I: Why not?

S: Did not. It wasn't mentioned.

[Application Question 29: What do we note from the interviewee's use of the word *it* in reference to his wife?]

I: She didn't bring it up?

S: No, sir.

I: You didn't bring it up?

S: No, sir. Did not.

I: Was your wife ever treated for any injuries at the local hospital? Do you ever recall taking your wife to the hospital?

S: For any injuries? Not as I know of.

[Application Question 30: What happened in the response above?]

I: Do you know who your wife's dentist was?

S: No, sir. I do not.

I: You don't know. Did you know whether she went to a dentist or not?

S: Uh, yes, she went to a dentist here, when she's here. Down in town if, if she ever did, I never did recall of her going to a dentist there. But, but here she went to a dentist, but I don't remember what dentist or what she had to do, whether it was a tooth pulled or filled or what.

[**Application Question 31:** How would you summarize what can be learned from the response above?]

I: You don't recall whether your wife had all of her teeth or not?

S: No, sir, I don't.

I: Okay. Do you remember her ever wearing dentures?

S: No, she did not.

I: She did not. She had all her teeth.

S: Had all of her teeth.

I: Okay. You don't remember her ever being treated for any broken bones or any other …

S: No, sir.

I: Problems?

S: No, sir.

I: Mr. _____, is there anything else you have to say about your wife's disappearance?

S: That's all I, uh, that I know.

[**Application Question 32:** How would you summarize the exchange above?]

I: Where do you think your wife is today?

S: The only thing that I know is, is that, she is assumed to be dead. But to know, like I said, don't know whether she's dead or not. The only way that I could, uh, pronounce that anybody was dead was to see 'em while they were dead. And I don't know, uh, I wouldn't say that she, she is. I wouldn't say she isn't, isn't dead, but I assume from all reports that she might be. I'll put it that way.

[**Application Question 33:** How would you summarize the response above?]

I: Well, how do you figure that? 'Cause earlier you told me you didn't know what her situation was.

S: Well, the, from what you said, the statement you give me. You give me a statement that, you said that you thought definitely she was dead. And that's what I …

I: You're basing your belief solely on what I said?

S: On, on what you said, that you, that you think that she's dead and if, with all the other reports, sounds logical.

I: Sounds logical now?

S: That's right. That she might be dead.

I: Sounds logical now that the tape recorder's on, that she sounds dead?

S: From what you, from what you said to me. I'm talking about from what you said to me.

I: But before I turned on this tape recorder, you didn't know what her status was?

S: Well, I don't. I really don't. I really don't.

I: But you think it's logical that she's dead?

S: Well, from what you said, there, from her not never reporting back to anybody and what you said. But as far as I know, I still say the same thing I said before. I don't know whether she's dead or not. Do not.

I: You didn't have anything to do with it?

S: Did not. Did not have nothing to do with it. Which, which …

[Application Question 34:   What can we gather from the interviewee's second attempt to ask a question?]

I: You didn't shoot your wife?

S: Did not.

I: You didn't stab your wife?

S: Did not.

I: Didn't strike your wife or beat her?

S: Did not

I: You didn't strangle your wife?

S: Did not. Did not. I'll tell you that with my hand up. Did not. Absolutely did not.

[Application Question 35:   What is different about the interviewee's answer to the question concerning strangling his wife, as opposed to shooting, stabbing, striking, or beating her? What could this difference indicate?]

I: Anything else?

S: That's all I know now.

[Application Question 36:   What does the qualifier "now" reveal?]

Summary

The consummate interviewer must be able to identify the indicators of the possibility of deception. However, it is also necessary for the interviewer to keep in mind that the changes in behavior are just that—changes in behavior. They are not in and of themselves proof positive the interviewee is deceptive. Only when the interviewee using falsification makes a mistake and reveals the truth, or through the undertakings of the interviewer makes an admission, can the interviewer know the truth. Through the interviewer's questioning and attentive abilities, the conduct of the interview is carried out in a planned, professional manner.

Chapter 3

Questioning for Quality Information

When I burn'd in desire to question them further,
they made themselves air, into which they vanish'd.
                                    —Shakespeare, *Macbeth*

Application Question 1: Before you begin to study the art of questioning,
answer the following: How would you evaluate
your questioning skills? What are your questioning strong points and weaknesses? How important is the role of effective questioning within
your profession role? What are the positive downstream consequences of an effective interview as
it relates to your responsibilities? What are the
negative downstream consequences?

Aspects of Questioning

Control

Control is the foundation on which the successful application of all questioning techniques and skills must rest. The interviewer must gain and continually maintain control of the interview. If the interviewer cannot maintain
control, then there is a good probability the interviewee will divert the process,
leading the interview in directions of his or her own choosing or, worse, becoming the interviewer.

The interview process always includes control: either the interviewer or the
interviewee controls the interview. But what is control? Within the interview
context, control is the ability to elicit a response from the interviewee. *Response* is the key element. The interviewer endeavors to determine what he or
she must do to produce the desired response from the interviewee. Before we
can get the *desired* response, we must be able to get *some* response.

The interesting point is that there will always be some response; the interviewee will always respond somehow. The critical issue is whether the inter-

viewee will respond as the interviewer wishes. Nothing happens in a vacuum. Everything we do (or don't do) has an effect on the interviewee. Consequently, control or power in the interview is derived from one's ability to persuade the interviewee to respond in the desired manner. The skilled interviewer endeavors to have the "power to" as an effective communicator, as opposed to having "power over," based on having a certain position—police officer, auditor, proprietary investigator, and so on. An interviewer who relies solely on having power over—deriving from a position they hold—is going to be ineffective and frustrated. Power over, also known as positional power, is a diminishing reality in the world today.

An interview is neither an argument nor a debate. The controlling arrow of power should be directed as follows:

Interviewer's Questions and Actions → Interviewee's Response

Responses from the interviewee can be weighted along a scale from 0 to 100. A response of 0 would be indicative of the interviewee who says, "I don't have anything to say to you. I want an attorney, union representative," and so on. He or she responds, but the response is terminal. Sometimes the response we get on this scale ranks as a 2, 3, 4, or 5. What is going on here? The interviewee is responding! The response may occur in the form of anger, such as hostile remarks about you or your agency, complaints about unjust or unfair treatment, and so on. As discouraging as these lower number indicators may seem initially, they still serve as responses. Any response is better than a 0. Here we have opportunity; we have options; we have a chance.

Unfortunately, an interviewer may react negatively to this type of response, that is, by becoming angry. Anger reflects a loss of self-control. Becoming angry amounts to giving control of one's emotions to the person who made you angry; this, of course, is the exact opposite of the goal—to control the interviewee's emotions. The interviewer who cannot control him- or herself cannot control the interviewee. (Rule: The interviewer never gets angry. While interviewers can portray anger, as an emotive producing technique, for example, we must never actually become angry.)

To return to our discussion of the response scale, however, even responses from reported victims may be less than 100. Though victims may willingly report most of what happened to them, there can still be certain details or kinds of information they are reluctant to share. For example, a fraud victim may describe everything that happened with the exception of a critical detail that may be of embarrassment to him or her. Here again, the interviewer's self-control, in terms of patience and tact, may be necessary for the satisfactory resolution of concealment on the part of the victim.

Our interview strategy, if diagrammed, should take the following form:

Interviewer	→	Interviewee
Question	→	Answer
Question	→	Answer

Should we move into a phase where the interviewee responds to a question with another question, or with a statement instead of an answer, chances are we are dealing with an individual who is becoming resistant and attempting to turn the arrow of power against the interviewer.

Exercise 3. Read the following transcript and answer the questions that follow.

Rick:	Another thing is that if, in fact, there is an arrest made. Even if it is just for suspicion. The first thing that always, since I've been maybe twelve years old. The first thing that always pops into my mind, before any questions were asked about who I am or anything. If I'm guilty or not, don't make no difference. The first thing that pops into my mind is, what kind of answer can I give this man without giving him nothing at all. That's all I'm thinking about. Regardless of what you ask. I'm always thinking what kind of answer can I give you without giving you nothing anyway. Just to give you something so that I can go on and you can go on. And the first thing that's always ever popped in my mind, up to this day—what kind of answer can I give you, to either satisfy you where you say, "This boy, this young man or this guy here is just not going to give us nothing. Go on." It's eluding a question with a question, but it's in answer form.
Interviewer:	But what would you do, answer a question with a question?
Rick:	Yeah. If you was to ask me about my past as far as, maybe, a few months ago. In the

past. "Well, where were you on the night of such and such?" "Well, to tell you the truth, you know, the only thing ..." And then you go off into something else. To hell with the question you just asked. Talk about something else, you know, or make a statement to something else.

- What tactics of a deceptive interviewee has Rick articulated in the transcript?
- What insights into the mind of the deceiver can you derive from Rick's explanation of his actions?
- What questioning options would the interviewer have at this point in the conduct of the interview in response to Rick's machinations?

Application Question 2: How would you describe your ability to control an interview? Have you ever become angry during the conduct of an interview? If so, what was it the interviewee said or did that made you angry? Do you have a tendency to objectify or personalize the issue that is the focus of the interview? Think of the best interview you have ever conducted. What enabled you to maintain control in that circumstance? Conversely, think of the most salient interview wherein you were not able to maintain control. What prevented you from maintaining control in that circumstance? What would you need to use the attributes you maintained in the best interview into the conduct of all interviews?

Plan

An interview is a planned procedure. Each interview involves the development of a plan. Certainly, the guilty or the guilty knowledge interviewee has a plan; hopefully, the interviewer will have one as well. Interviewers often take the attitude that preinterview planning is time-consuming and unnecessary. Nothing could be further from reality.

If there is a plan, then once the interview begins, the interviewer has one thing left to do—implement the plan. Even if it becomes necessary to modify or alter the plan once the interview has begun, the interviewer at least has a basis on which to exercise options. If there is no plan, an additional step is required—develop a plan. Simply stated, it is easier to do one thing at a time than it is to do two things at once, as the following diagram suggests.

Interviewer with no plan	Interviewee with a plan
Develop plan	Implement plan
Implement plan	

The interviewer who begins an interview with no plan gives the interviewee a distinct advantage. But what factors should be considered in preinterview planning?

What do we know about the circumstance? It is critical the interviewer be thoroughly familiar with the substance of the issue at hand. Once the interview begins, the interviewer who lacks a working knowledge of the issue will have difficulty identifying discrepancies or omissions in the interviewee's account. Additionally, there is a tendency for the uninformed interviewer to look at paper instead of people. Once the interview begins, all new information is going to come from the interviewee, not from a file folder.

What do we know about the interviewee? To whatever extent is possible, it is critical the interviewer know everything possible concerning the interviewee. Information might at first glance seem insignificant could ultimately prove invaluable for gaining insight into the interviewee and his or her relationship to the circumstance under inquiry. Additionally, the interviewer's plan will be developed along lines directly suggested by the knowledge gained in reference to the interviewee.

What do we know about the interviewer? As an interviewer, you must be aware of your strengths and weaknesses, especially during stressful situations. Are you impatient or long suffering? Do you easily get frustrated, or do you maintain your composure? Can you maintain a train of thought during tense situations, or do you find it difficult to stay outwardly focused?

Questioning: The Instruments of Inquiry

In the process of inquiring and persuading, nothing is more important than the ability to question. Voltaire said, "Judge of a man by his questions rather than by his answers." Certainly, an interviewer will be judged by his or her questions. Socrates said, "Just look at my question; how plain and simple it is." That is the point, to the capable interviewer: Questions are simple, but to the deceptive interviewee answers are not so simple.

We shall discover that by far the great majority of inquiries are made with a single questioning strategy. It is not a bad strategy, but neither is it the only strategy available. Sometimes the interviewer will not benefit by its utilization because that strategy will not work in a particular circumstance. As we have addressed previously, the interviewer who can reach into the tackle box of questioning techniques and use each kind effectively at the appropriate point within the interview has a greater chance of success because he or she can adjust to the shifting environment of the interview (read: interviewee) itself.

To identify the various questions available, as well as their strong points and drawbacks, we use an excerpt from a transcript of an actual interview. Those questioning strategies used in the interview will be highlighted within the context of the interview, and those that are not used, although appropriate, will be addressed at specific points. (All the names and identifying information mentioned in the following excerpt have been changed.)

I: I guess this thing is working … Ah, my name is Jim Jones. I'm a homicide detective that's investigating the death of Mary Turner. And … uh … I understand that you were a friend of hers.

S: I was … I lived with her for two years, and we were engaged for a while. We separated in July. And basically … the last time I saw her personally was about two weeks ago when I saw her down at Harborhome.

Comment 1

Even in this "prior to questioning" stage of the interview, the interviewer would note the terms *basically* and *personally*. Does "the last time I saw her personally" mean the last time he saw her? Does *basically* indicate this is most — but not all — of the narrative? As noted in Chapter 2, always pay attention to the point where the interviewee loses the ability to commit to his or her own narrative through the use of modifiers or qualifiers.

I: Okay, let me get your full name, sir.

S: Daniel.

I: D-a-n-i …

S: D-a-n-i-e-l … E. You want an initial or what?

I: Full name.

S: Edwards.

I: E-d …

S: W-a-r-d-s.

I: How old are you?

S: I'm forty-two.

I: And your date of birth?

S: 3/28/46 ... 3/28/46 ... March 28, 1946.

I: And your home address?

S: 2834 Lake Shore.

I: Phone?

S: 555-1389.

I: Your business phone?

Closed-Ended Questions

Comment 2

Up to this point in the interview we have observed *closed-ended questions.* The most common type of question, closed-ended questions tend to require an answer of "yes" or "no," or a brief response at most. They can be useful for verifying information. Additionally, closed-ended questions do not provide for extended responses and, as a rule, do not cause the interviewee to relax. The tempo of the interview will be:

Question	*Answer*	*Stop*
Question	*Answer*	*Stop*

We notice after each closed-ended question the interviewee provides an answer and then stops talking. If the interviewer's plan is to use a sequence of questions intended to encourage the interviewee to relax and thus enhance response, this series of closed-ended questions will be counterproductive to that goal. Some examples of closed-ended questions are:

- Do you know who authorized the contract?
- Is this all you know about the awarding of the contract?
- Are you telling me the truth?
- Did you alter the records?

Evaluate your own questioning history to determine if you rely heavily on closed-ended questions.

S: Um ... I actually don't know that—I'm with Cape Point Ambulatory. Sometimes I'm at Pamonna.

I: Um ... How did you and Mary meet? How did you all become friends?

Comment 3

The foregoing excerpt is an example of asking two questions. Before the interviewee can answer the first question, a second question has been posed. These questions can represent two distinct areas to explore: how they met and how they became friends. Avoid the common tendency to pose multiple questions. Ask one question at a time, wait, let the interviewee answer that question, and then proceed.

> S: Well, actually, I met her a long time ago … She came in professionally … I took care of her, and then, later on, I saw her again when I was shopping with my mother buying some … you know … clothes, and then after that … you know … we just started talking and I asked her out. I took her out to lunch, and we went out several times after that and started to like each other and started to spend a lot more time seeing each other. We just started seeing each other and that was basically it, you know.
>
> I: And how long did you see each other?
>
> S: You mean our relationship?
>
> I: Uh-huh.
>
> S: About two years.
>
> I: Tell me about the period of time when you were engaged.

Application Question 3: In the conduct of an interview, what percentage of your questions are closed questions? Is your utilization of closed questions appropriate, too high, or too low? Do you think you would be able to conduct a productive interview if you limited yourself to only being able to ask five closed questions?

Open-Ended Questions

Comment 4

The foregoing is an example of an *open-ended question*. An open-ended question will normally provoke a more extended answer that includes more details. The interviewee is required to provide a narrative. The open-ended question can serve the interviewer in gaining more insight into the interviewee. Instead of asking the series of closed-ended questions that initiated the interview, the interviewer could have chosen to start with the open-ended question: "Tell me about yourself."

Here, the open ended question can serve several purposes:

- to encourage the interviewee to respond;
- to gain insight into the interviewee, based on how he or she describes him- or herself;
- to aid the interviewee in relaxing, if appropriate.

Open-ended questions tend to be rare occurrences in the interview process. They are, in fact, more challenging for the interviewer to incorporate, but the results they produce are more than worth the effort. Some examples of open-ended questions would be:

- What were the circumstances involving the awarding of the contract?
- How did you get from work to the bar?
- Why did you leave work early on that particular day?
- Could you explain to me the circumstances that led to the cancellation of the loan?
- Would you begin with the time you got to work and tell me everything that happened?

With an open question, the interviewee will tend to open up, revealing information about him- or herself and the circumstances. With each word, we learn more about the interviewee. On the other hand, always be alerted by the interviewee who responds to an open-ended question in the following manner.

I: Could you tell me what happened from the time you opened up the deposit bag until you noticed that the deposit was $2,500 short?

S: What do you want to know?

In this exchange, the interviewee answers the question with another question. He wants specific or salient points to be identified. He is saying, in effect, "You tell me what is important to you so that I can see your cards and you will not see mine."

The interviewer should answer as follows, eliciting the following response:

I: Everything.

S: Well, you ask me the questions and I will give you the answers.

The interviewee would prefer the interviewer to ask revealing, closed-ended questions. But the interviewer, fully in control, responds otherwise.

I: Until you have explained to me what happened, I do not have any questions to ask you. I mean, that is not that difficult is it?

At this point the interviewer will transition into silence. As an interviewer, you should learn to become comfortable with silence. Silence does not mean nothing is being communicated. Wait until the interviewee answers. Let silence and the passing of time work toward your advantage.

Evaluate your past interviewing history and consider those times when open-ended questions might have better served you. It will assist you to actually make a list of the open-ended questions that are appropriate to an interviewing circumstance prior to questioning the interviewee. Familiarize yourself with those questions and keep them in mind during the conduct of the interview.

S: Yeah. This happened in, um, ... more or less in June. She wanted to get married. She had lived in my house and she moved out, back to her apartment, over there. We stayed over there for a while. But then ... ah ... she wanted to get married. And I sort of wanted to get married, but I wasn't quite ready for it. And I ... ah ... basically she told me she wanted to be with me on July nineteenth, and I couldn't settle for that date because at that time I was going through a bad situation at work and I was deciding if I was going to stay at Mantella Acute Care, where I was for the last three or four years, or whether my group, which runs the Mantella — the unit — would lose their contract with Wakus Hospital, and if they did, then I would have to go — Mantella and I could not go with another group in order to keep working. So, I needed some more time to think. She said July the nineteenth. So I said, I can't do that. So she broke up with me, and I said okay, and I didn't see her since then.

I: You haven't seen her at all since July the nineteenth?

S: No, I haven't seen her at all except when I saw her at the lounge at Harborhome with her boyfriend on Saturday nights. It was two weeks ago and ... three weeks ago.

I: After you broke up on July the nineteenth. Right?

S: No, not July the nineteenth. It was the first of July that we broke up.

I: And you didn't see her until you saw her a couple weeks ago at Harborhome. Did you talk to her on the phone?

If we were to compare an interviewee to a meal, open questions would be the main entree. All of the other questioning types are side dishes. The side dishes are there to enhance the meal. As tempting as it may be, do not try to make a meal out of a side dish.

Application Question 4: How often do you ask open questions? Do you hesitate to use open questions for fear of losing control of the interview? How often do you apply open questions to the interview process? Are you able to apply the effective use of open questions with closed questions?

Connecting Questions

Comment 5

The interviewer's last question in the foregoing is an example of a *connecting question*. As its name suggests, this type of question serves to connect details and events. The first sentence in the sequence is actually a summary of what the interviewee had previously stated. The connecting question follows, expanding the topic of the meeting at Harborhome to include any telephone conversations held prior to or after that meeting.

The connecting-question sequence allows the interviewer to peel back the narrative, layer by layer, to penetrate more deeply into its details and events.

> S: Oh, yeah, I called her up about three weeks ago and called her up about two weeks ago. The first time I called her I was real sad and just talked to her. And the second time I called her up and just wanted to see how she was doing. She seemed real happy and everything. I told her about the tape I wanted to get her and she said okay, so I went to buy the tape, and I left it for her at work and told her girlfriend that was it. It was a tape of Anita Baker and that was it. You know.
>
> I: Do you have a key to her apartment?

Comment 6

In the interviewee's answer to this last, closed-ended question, we can see one of the advantages to using such questions. What we notice is the interviewee never actually answers the question about having a key to her apartment when he responds, "I did a long time ago, but she took it back when we broke up." (It is very difficult for a deceptive interviewee to answer simply "no" to a closed question.) As we demonstrated in our diagram earlier, the power-related questioning should proceed as follows:

Question → *Answer*

Question → *Answer*

But here we observe the following sequence: Question → Statement.

"Do you have a key to her apartment?" is a closed-ended question. It need only be answered with a "yes" or a "no," but the response is a statement. A similar sequence occurs later in the interview.

    I: Did you kill her?

    S: What are you asking me that for?

Here we have a closed-ended question answered with another question:

Question → Question

Why is this question answered with a question when all the interviewee has to say is "no"? Questions of this type answered with anything other than "no" tend to get the interviewer thinking in terms of "yes"—and in terms of a deceptive interviewee.

Let's move on to a different interview, which will illustrate several important points. As you read the following dialogue, note the interviewer's use of closed-ended questions, the interviewee's attempts to ask the questions, the interviewee answering a question with a question, and the interviewee's difficulty in simply answering, "no."

    I: Do you have a girlfriend?

    S: Do I have a girlfriend? I have a wife. I've been married five years.

    I: Now, a lot of people that are married have girlfriends.

    S: If I had a girlfriend, what's that got to do with a breaking-and-entering anyway?

    I: Okay, we'll get to that. Herman, do you know a girl named Sandra?

    S: I ... I ... I might know somebody named Sandra.

    I: You might? You do or you don't?

    S: I might.

    I: Have you ever dated a girl named Sandra?

    S: I might have; I don't remember.

    I: I told you when I came in here, I had some information, Herman. I am just a fact finder. This information that I have, I'm not trying to threaten you or anything.

    S: Are you charging me with something?

    I: I'm telling you I called you up here to talk to you. There's a matter we need to straighten out. It's to your benefit. That's why I called you up here.

    S: What happened again?

    I: I'm investigating a break-in on Morriston. Do you know the location? Do you know where Morriston is located?

    S: No, I sure don't.

I: You don't?

S: Sure don't.

I: Do you know Sandra?

S: I've heard the name before.

I: Have you dated Sandra?

S: Like I said, I'm married.

I: That doesn't have anything to do with what I'm asking you.

S: I might have seen her a couple of times. I wouldn't call it dating.

I: A lot of married men have mistresses on the side. Am I right?

S: I don't know about a lot of other married men.

I: No, I'm just telling you—a lot of married men do date on the side. Is that correct? That's just the facts of life.

S: They might. I don't know. I've been happily married.

I: You've been happily married.

S: Five years.

I: About five years. And you never cut out on your wife?

S: No, I can't say that I have.

Comment 7

What conclusion can the interviewer draw from such a response as "I can't *say* that I have"? The interviewer should note the interviewee did not claim he had *not* "cut out on" his wife but, rather, he could not *say* he had done so. Do not interpret a response of this type as a denial. Listen to every word!

We return to our initial interview.

I: Do you have a key to her apartment?

S: I did a long time ago, but she took it back when we broke up.

I: You didn't keep a copy of it?

S: No, I don't. I don't. I'm not like that. She said when we broke up, and I agreed with her.

I: You took this tape to her job at June Fairs, didn't you?

Application Question 5: Have you ever consciously asked connecting questions in an interview you have conducted? How could connecting questions apply within your interviewing area of responsibility? How could you incorporate open, closed, and connecting questions into the conduct of your interviews?

Positive-Reaction Questions

Comment 8

The foregoing excerpt offers an example of a *tag question*. Tag questions serve several purposes, including gaining agreement from the interviewee. Additionally, tag questions identify any barrier to cooperation on the part of the interviewee, if one exists. Consequently, if the interviewer can determine what is preventing the interviewee from moving into the "willing" chair, he or she can address that concern and possibly remove the barrier. The interviewee's concern can be addressed through one or more of the available rationalization and persuasion techniques.

Tag questions have a double-play effect: seeking the interviewee's agreement at the beginning, then using the anchor in the question's to elicit a reaction from the interviewee. Examples of tag questions are:

- You know who authorized the contract, do you not?
- You would rather tell the truth in this matter than have it hanging over your head, wouldn't you?
- The cutbacks have resulted in you having to take on the job responsibilities of two other people, hasn't it?

Tag questions can also be structured with the anchor portion placed at the beginning. By being able to use both forms, the interviewer can minimize the possibility of the interviewee becoming aware of the process. Examples of this form of tag question would be:

- Isn't it true you knew there was a discrepancy before the audit began?
- Don't you believe it would be better just to put all of the details on the table?

The interviewer can use tag questioning with neutral third parties, possible co-conspirators, as well as targets of an inquiry.

I: Mary, a loyal employee, is going to do what is in the best interest of the company, isn't she?

S: Yes, but you don't want to get your friend in trouble if they haven't done anything wrong.

Here the interviewee has revealed her concern is with what will happen to her friend, who she suspects of wrong doing but has no proof, if she elects to cooperate. This gives the interviewer an opportunity to react and resolve. Perhaps he would respond in this manner:

Mary, I want you to know that you cannot get your friend in trouble. If you have a suspicion, tell me and I will inquire into it. If your friend has done nothing wrong, that is exactly what it will show. No one ever got in trouble because someone had a suspicion. If your friend is involved in something, then we can keep this from getting any worse. So Mary, you see that you cannot hurt your friend. Only your friend can do that. But, Mary, you can certainly help your friend by assisting in showing that your friend has done nothing wrong.

Another option for the interviewer could be as story: "Mary, you know, you remind me of a woman I was working with the other day. She was concerned about her friend, as any good person would be, but she was also concerned about her company, as any loyal employee would be." Giving some consideration to the application and formation of questions designed to provoke a positive reaction and/or to identify barriers to cooperation would be to the interviewer's advantage. Another attribute of tag questions is they allow the interviewer to transcend the fear of confession. At the appropriate point within the interview, the interviewer can ask, "Jim, you intended to place all of the money back as soon as you got your mother past her medical crisis, didn't you?" In this case, all Jim has to do is agree with the interviewer rather than confess.

Use caution and make sure you are not asking a tag question when you should be asking a closed question. For example, there is a great deal of difference between, "You didn't take the money did you?" and "Did you take the money?" In the first case, it is much easier for the interviewee to reply deceptively than it is in the second. This type of questioning error happens a lot. Don't let it happen to you.

However, if you *want* to show the interviewee as a liar, ask a tag question about something you know to be true and make it easy for the interviewee to respond deceptively. For example, you know the interviewee is on the board of another company doing business with the firm in which he is employed. Among other things, this is a violation of policy and a conflict of interest. To show him as a deceiver you might want to consider asking, "Now you are not on the board of any company currently doing business with _____ Industries are you?"

I: You took this tape to her job at June Fairs, didn't you?
S: Yes sir, at Shopping Square.
I: When was that?
S: That was on Monday.
I: Did you talk to her at that time?

> S: No, I didn't because she wasn't working. So, I left it with a girl who works in her department.
>
> I: Any idea who she was?
>
> S: No, just some girl.
>
> I: What was the significance of the tape?

[later in the interview]

> I: During your two-year relationship with Mary, did you ever have a physical relationship ... er ... a physical confrontation?
>
> S: Oh, we had our arguments ... We had our arguments.

Application Question 6: Have you ever consciously asked a tag question during the conduct of an interview? How do you think this questioning option would apply to the conduct of your interviews? Do you think you have ever asked a tag question, thinking you were asking a closed question? How could you incorporate open, closed, connecting, and positive-reaction questions to your interviewing responsibilities?

Clarifying Questions

Comment 9

This point in the interview offers an excellent opportunity for a *clarifying question*. The clarifying question is used to encourage the interviewee to expand on an undefined portion of his or her narrative. The interviewee has just stated, "We had our arguments." Since the interviewer does not yet know what the interviewee means by an "argument," it is an undefined term at this point. In listening to the interviewee's statement, the interviewer would note the terms *we* and *our*, suggesting the involvement of both parties, rather than a one-sided perspective, as well as the plural "arguments," indicating more than one such incident.

Examples of clarifying questions this interviewer might respond with:

- You said, "We had our arguments," tell me more.
- You said, "We had our arguments," give me an example.

Clarifying questions can follow easily after open-ended questions.

> I: But did you ever beat her?
>
> S: No, I never beat her. I held her hands ... you know ... because she would ... she would start yelling things, but I never ...

I: You never struck her in the face?

S: No, I never struck her in the face. I held her. I put her down. I said "that's enough." Let's stop fighting ... you know ... that was it.

Application Question 7: Do you have a tendency to assume you understand what the interviewee means when he or she utilizes nonspecific terms? Are you willing to probe for specificity? If so, what questioning techniques have you used to probe within a specific area?

Forced-Choice Questions

Comment 10

At this point in the interview, the interviewer could consider using a *forced-choice question*. The forced-choice question requires an answer chosen from among two or more possible responses. Normally, a forced-choice question will be used *after* the establishment of some fact or circumstance. Here, the interviewee has indicated he "never struck her in the face," but he has not indicated he never struck her at all. Additionally, with the phrase "let's stop fighting," he has indicated that they fought.

The forced-choice question can enable the interviewer to press for additional, specific disclosures. Examples of forced-choice questions the interviewer might ask here are:

- When you fought, was it because of something you did that made her mad, or something she did that made you mad?
- When you "put her down," was it before or after she had struck you?

Forced-choice questions are similar to leading questions. The primary difference is whether a certain fact or circumstance has already been established.

I: That's not what other people had to say about you.

Comment 11

The statement above is *confrontational*. Note it does not end in a question mark. It is not, in fact, a question, yet it will elicit a response.

Here, the interviewee is confronted with a contradiction between what he has stated and other information the interviewer has obtained. The interviewer can now observe how the interviewee responds to the confrontation. His answer could be very revealing.

> S: Well … you know. I … I could only say so much … you
>   know … but I'm not that type of person … I don't … I
>   don't … most of the time.

Note this very weak and unsupported denial. The interviewee tells the interviewer he "could only say so much … you know." The interviewer concludes there is more to be said than the interviewee has elected to say. Additionally, the interviewer notices the associated changes in speech pattern, including pauses, interjections of "you know" and repetitions of "I don't." Also, the interviewee qualifies his answer by adding the phrase "most of the time," indicating there has been other times when what he has implied was not the case. Again — and this is always the key concept — there is a *change*. What does the confrontational statement bring out in the interviewee we haven't seen before?

Application Question 8: In what interviewing circumstances would the application of forced-choice questions be applicable for you? At what level of attentiveness do you think the interviewer must be operating to use forced-choice questions? Do you believe that you are able to consistently maintain focus within the conduct of the interview to employ forced-choice questions?

Exercise 4: Review this interview transcript from the beginning and note those places where this same sequence of "you know," "I don't … I don't" has occurred. Are there other sections of the interviewee's narrative where modifiers appeared? What connection can you draw?

Control Questions

Comment 12

Now would be an appropriate time in the interview process to evaluate the interviewee's truthfulness. The interviewer can attempt such verification through the use of *control questions*. Control questions can serve to assess in the determination of the interviewee's:

- willingness to make a statement against his or her own self-interest;
- response in terms of a providing a rationale for the act;
- opinion regarding punishment for the act;
- reaction to an expression of disbelief by the interviewer.

The following situation provides an opportunity to examine the use of control questions.

An interviewer is making inquiry into a situation involving possible "internal shrinkage" (losses due to theft by employees) from the men's department of a clothing store. There are three people who work in that department. Sometimes all three employees are working there at once; sometimes two employees are working, and often just one is working at any particular time. The interviewer is attempting to determine whether interviewee one, two, three, or any combination thereof might be responsible for the losses.

In questioning each of these individuals privately, the interviewer may elect to use a certain sequence of questions. These questions are posed in a manner that suggests the interviewer is thinking out loud or is simply wondering. The interviewer need not ask these questions in any particular order, nor do they have to follow directly one after another. However, the interviewer is attending closely to the interviewee's *response* to each question. Is the response indicative of a defensive interviewee or of one who is not at all defensive?

> I: Jim, I was just wondering, of all those who work in the men's department, who *could* take the money or the merchandise? I am not asking you who did do it. I am only wondering who could do it.

[The interviewee might answer as follows:]

> S: Well, if property is missing from the department, then, if you are asking who could have done it, it could be any of us three. I could do it, David could do it, or Frank could do it. We are there at times alone and we each work through the same computer.

This answer tends to indicate a truthful individual. He is willing to implicate himself as a possible suspect. He does not appear to be threatened by the recognition that he could be considered responsible for the thefts, nor is he reluctant to admit he had the opportunity to commit them.

On the other hand, the interviewee could have answered the same question by saying, "It could be David, or it could be Frank. They are both there alone, and each works out of the same computer, and each handles returned merchandise. So it could be either one." This is the response of an interviewee who, despite all things being equal, has elected not to include himself as a possible suspect. He is removing himself from any possibility of being considered involved and is apparently threatened by any suggestion of such involvement. The interviewer continues his questioning of Jim.

> I: Jim, I wonder *why* someone would do this: Why take money or merchandise from the store?
> S: I think he would do it because he is a thief. I mean, if somebody gives a person a job and puts him in a position of trust

and then that guy turns around and steals from him, … well, he is just a crook.

This response is indicative of a truthful interviewee. The reason he gives for someone's stealing is that such a person is a "thief," a "crook." He uses the term *steals*, and he is firm in his willingness to condemn the individual for such behavior. However, the interviewee might have answered, "Maybe he did it because he needed the money. Maybe his mother was sick, or he had something come up that he just couldn't cover." This response is, in effect, a rationalization for the act, suggesting hypothetical reasons for stealing. Rather than the thief being condemned, the interviewee speculates about justifiable reasons for the act.

> I: Jim, *what do you think should happen* to someone who would do this?
>
> S: Well, I don't know what the penalty for doing it is, but whatever it calls for, they ought to give it to him and throw the key away.

This interviewee responds by calling for punishment. There is a penalty for this act, and the penalty should be paid. The interviewee is not threatened by the idea of punishment because it doesn't apply to him. However, the interviewee might have answered, "I think they should let him pay the money back, or they could take it out of his pay. Maybe they should let the person go. I think the person needs help." In this response we hear, not a call for punishment but a call for amnesty. The idea of a penalty for the act is apparently threatening. Now the interviewer has the option of asking the following type of question.

> I: Jim, *what would you say if I indicated to you that I don't believe you?*
>
> S: [angrily] What do you mean, you don't believe me?! You asked me about this and I told you. If you don't know the truth, then I don't think you should be the person in here talking to me. And I'll tell you this, I don't like being called a liar!

This is the response of an interviewee who takes what the interviewer says *personally*. This person is emotionally involved; he is upset. We tend to feel good about this interviewee, unlike one who replies, "Hey, that's your problem. You can believe me if you want. That's up to you. I don't care." This is not the response of an interviewee who takes the interviewer's insinuation personally. He isn't angry because, to him, this is "your problem," not his. The insinuation he is a liar does not bother him. He already "knows" he is.

Still, the interviewer, who is always willing to give the interviewee the benefit of a doubt, pursues the matter.

> I: Wait now, Jim. I didn't say that I didn't believe you; I just asked how that would you say. That does not make you mad does it?
>
> S: [still upset] Yeah, that made me mad. I'm telling you the truth, and I want you to know that I am not a liar.

For this interviewee, the situation is still personal. He continues to be involved, unlike the interviewee who responds, "No, it doesn't make me mad. I know you are just doing your job." This interviewee is revealing a great deal by his response. He does not take these two questions personally. He is willing to let you know he understands your position, and that "you are just doing your job." The implication, however, is that he is just doing *his* job. Simply stated, your job is to get to the truth, and his job is to keep it from you. It is not personal; it is professional. In his own way, he is inadvertently advising, "Don't take my deception personally. This is a job, a professional matter."

When you are using control questions, unless the interviewee's response is clearly an indication of the possibility of deception, put the response in your mental "response of an honest interviewee" column. Err on the side of caution. Whenever there is doubt with regard to any of the interviewee's verbal, vocal, or nonverbal behavior, give the benefit of the doubt to the interviewee.

There are a multitude of control questions to draw from; however, if the interviewer cannot get an adequate "read" on the interviewee from three or four questions, then twelve or fourteen are not going to prove to be more effective. There is a point of diminishing returns with regard to the utilization of control questions, and that limit does not take long to reach.

Exercise 5. Read the following interview excerpt and answer the application questions that follow:

> Rick: When we get a write-up in here, for example. We go before a disciplinary committee—just like a court. We've got our story made up before we go in there. We know we're guilty and we know they're going to find us guilty, no matter what we say. But still, when we walk in there he's got a charge right on paper. And a lot of times it depends on how the guy talks to you. Biggest thing is, here you are going before a board—"This officer says that you've done this." "I didn't do that. I don't know

	what he's talking about. He's a liar. I was down the hall there with my buddies." See you're prepared for what is coming. But now if the guy is sitting there and you've got somebody decent on that board, that you've dealt with, you'll open up to him. You'll talk to him man to man.
Interviewer:	Let's take the situation you were talking about. You've got your story. You're going to tell them that you were down the hall with your buddies. You tell them that and the guy on the board looks at you and says, "I don't believe you." He isn't mad, he just tells you that he does not believe you. But let's say that you get written up and you're in there and you really were down the hall with your buddies. And you tell him that. And the guy looks at you and says, "I don't believe you." Is there any difference in the way you feel when you are telling the truth and you are not telling the truth?
Rick:	When you tell the truth and you're getting the same punishment, and that's what it is. The man sits there and says, "I don't believe you, I've done heard that before." And he gives you the same punishment as if you did it, you got but one recourse—that's to appeal his decision.
Interviewer:	If you know what you're telling him is not the truth, and he says, "I don't believe you"—what then?
Rick:	You just go on. You've got to finish that role.
Interviewer:	If you know what you're telling him is the truth, and then he says, "I don't believe you"—does that bother you more?
John:	Sure.
Application Question 9:	Relate Rick and John's responses to the concept of the functionality of control questions. What were their different reactions when they were deceptive and when they were truthful to the same ques-

tion? What is the significance of the words, "You've got to finish that role" to the mindset of the deceptive interviewee? Within your interviewing areas of responsibility, how would control questions apply? Would control questions have no place in your interviewing techniques options? If so, why? In your mind, how do you think you would respond to control questions if you were innocent of any wrong doing? What if you were guilty?

Secondary Questions

Comment 13

We now utilize an alternative interview scenario to assess the usefulness of *secondary questions.* Secondary questions work in conjunction with open questions. They can be used to follow up on and clarify information we already have. These questions are often based on the interviewee's response to a prior question. There are various options for the application of secondary questions or statements—they need not be limited to the interrogatory form or always end with a question mark.

Secondary questions can include sounds, sights, as well as actual words. Their advantage lies in keeping the interviewee's narrative stream flowing and in encouraging more interviewee disclosure without having to ask additional questions. When using secondary questions, the interviewer should make sure to:

- Establish comfortable eye contact.
- Give soft, rhythmic, and slow vocal feedback: Um huh, uh huh. This is a very pleasing sound to someone who is talking to you. It indicates, "I am listening. This is interesting to me. Please go on."
- The interviewer should nod his or her head slightly.
- Listen for the communication marker that indicates the speaker is coming to a stop in what they have to say. His or her voice and words will become more pronounced, and there will be a change in tempo. Usually it will speed up, but not always. Just notice the change.
- Repeat the last sentence (or salient portions thereof) the interviewee said before he or she ceased talking.

Comment 14

> I: Okay. Well, we can talk about this. Let's go over this a little
>   bit. From the beginning, okay? And what I'd like you to do
>   is go over what happened yesterday. And about the time that
>   you got the baby-sitter over—Priscilla came over to baby-
>   sit. And what happened from there.
>
> S: What happened, uh, was, I really didn't need Priscilla. Be-
>   cause my boyfriend had come over.

Here is the first example of a *secondary question/statement*. It is known as
the *reflective probe*. Once the interviewee stopped talking, the interviewer
merely repeated the salient portion of the last response: "You really didn't need
Priscilla." This type of repetition prompts the interviewee to respond in the
affirmative or the negative, depending on the direction of the conversation,
and to add more information to the previous response. During the interview,
the interviewer has been nodding his head as the interviewee speaks, and he
has established good, comfortable eye contact with her. This action supports
and enhances his use of secondary questions.

> S: No. But I didn't have a chance to tell her that.
>
> I: Uh huh.

The interviewer will want to cycle through the process—open question,
active listening, repeat the communication marker—two but no more than
three times before transitioning into the next form of secondary questions.
While this communication strategy is most effective for encouraging the interviewee to respond, if the interviewer stays with the technique too long, the
interviewee will become conscious of what is going on and will likely become
irritated and defensive. Always be able to change up your questioning pitches
so the interviewee does not consciously discern a pattern.

Comment 15

This "uh huh" is another form of secondary response, one that involves
sounds, not words. This sound assures the interviewee the interviewer is listening, he is involved and attentive. By its very nature as an affirmation, such
a sound will tend to keep the interviewee's narrative stream *flowing*. An open-
ended question supported by a series of secondary responses constitutes an
excellent strategy for enhancing the interviewee's response.

> S: I had made … I had called her and asked if she would baby-
>   sit. And she came over. Let's see, my boyfriend had already
>   arrived. And he wanted to spend the night. I said, "Fine."

Therefore, if he was going to be spending the night, then I wouldn't need Priscilla, right?

I: Right.

S: But she came over. And I said, "I have to leave." About … I have to work.

I: Uh huh.

S: I have to be there about six-thirty.

I: About six-thirty.

S: Yeah. Start work at seven. Get prepared.

I: Uh huh.

S: So, I assume, she … when I left with my boyfriend, Curtis _____ I left; they were there. Jason was being taken care of by Curtis. He was making supper for him. He was making some, some spaghetti or something. And I left. I don't know when Priscilla left the house.

I: You don't know when Priscilla left the house.

S: No. I don't know when she left my house. I haven't talked to her since. God!

I: Where was … what time did you come home?

S: I, I work from seven to around midnight—twelve-thirty. So I got home that particular Monday morning about one A.M.

I: About one A.M.

S: Yeah.

I: What happened when you got home?

S: What happened when I, when I arrived home? Well, I come in the door, you know, as I usually do. Put down my purse. Fix myself some milk or something to drink. And went into the bedroom, and Curtis was still awake. And I said, "How was Jason?" And he said, "Well, he was sort of temperamental today."

Comment 16

There is much we should be aware of in this response from the interviewee. Notice the verb tense the interviewee uses: "come," "put," and "fix." These are all present tense verbs. Be aware of the circumstances under which an interviewee begins to speak of a past occurrence as if it were happening right then. Particular note should be taken of a verb tense shift signaling a narrative *change,* as when this interviewee abruptly begins to speak as if what has already happened is actually occurring in the present. This behavior change provides an excellent area in which to return with further inquiry to explore both the details and the interviewee's reaction to the additional probing in that particular area. Additionally, the interviewer would note she began this particular response with a question.

I: Uh huh.

S: "And threw his supper around on the floor. And was just being, you know, very nasty." So I said, "Well, I'll have to go in and see what happened here." And I went into Jason's room. He was asleep. I woke him up. I said, "What did you do?"

I: Uh huh.

S: And he said, "Nothing, Mom. Nothing. I didn't do anything." And I said, "Well, Curtis told me you threw your supper on the floor." And he denied it and denied it. And I said, "Now, look, I know you did it. Why would Curtis lie?" And I did spank him, on the butt. I did not sling him around.

Comment 17

Be alert to an interviewee's response that includes information about what did *not* happen in response to an open question, "What happened?" (If it did not happen, why voluntarily bring it up?) Again, this dynamic can serve to alert the interviewer of another area in which to focus amplifying questions and to probe for details and specifics.

S: But I spanked him strongly, moderately on the butt. He was crying. And I told him to shut up and go to sleep. And that I would deal with him in the morning as to some extra form of punishment. Or see how I felt about it in the morning. Or just let it ride. Because he has been being very testy, very testy lately. He was making it difficult, really, to get up, to go to your job.

Comment 18

Notice the use of the pronoun *your*. Here the interviewee is talking about her own circumstances as if they were that of the interviewer (yours), not her own. Psychologically, she is removing herself from the arena of involvement and responsibility. It is as if she were in the ballpark but not in the ball game. The interviewer has to get her into the game. The pronoun *I* implies personal involvement and responsibility. Here, however, it would be enough for the interviewer to note that this pronoun change has occurred and return to that point with additional questions at the appropriate time.

S: To worry about him all day. It was just, very much. He was being a problem.

I: Uh huh.

S: On purpose sometimes. But, I mean, I loved him very much. He was my kid.

Comment 19

One option for the interviewer to consider at this point would be using a *leading question*. Such a strategy entails incorporating into the question a fact or a circumstance that has not been established within the dialogue between interviewer and the interviewee up to this point. If, in answering, the interviewee does not challenge the implicit assumption, then that fact or circumstance will be indirectly established. The question is designed to focus the interviewee's attention on peripheral issues, thus minimizing the importance of the assumption. Consequently, the response from the interviewee may be less guarded. An interviewer who can incorporate leading questions into the dialogue is able to stay one or two moves ahead of the interviewee in the conduct of the interview. In the interview we are now analyzing, the interviewer could have selected one of the following questions.

I: Was it when Curtis told you about the supper or when you saw the food on the floor that you got upset? (In answering, the interviewee would establish indirectly that she had indeed become upset.)

I: Was Jason's having thrown this food on the floor more upsetting to you or less upsetting to you than some of the other things he had done? (In answering this question, the interviewee would acknowledge both being upset and the existence of additional things the child had done to upset her.)

Other interview situations will provide other examples of leading questions, such as, "When you noticed the inappropriate overrides was it before or after the midyear audit?" Prior to this question, there would have been no discussion about the interviewee having noticed the inappropriate overrides. To supply the correct time, the interviewee must acknowledge to having noticed the overrides. Another leading question might be: "Do you immediately notify your supervisor when you authorize overrides in her name or do you wait until a subsequent account review meeting to make notification?" Prior to this question, there would have been no discussion about the interviewee's authorizing overrides by signing his supervisor's name. To answer simply in the affirmative regarding when or if the notification is made reveals the intervie-wee did in fact sign the supervisor's name to the overrides.

Application Question 10: Have you ever noticed a person using secondary question dynamics within the context of a nor-mal conversation—slowing nodding their head and providing vocal feedback? Think of the per-son you most enjoy talking to. What is his or her vocal and nonverbal demeanor when you are conversing? Does this person's behavior encour-age you to continue? Can you see the advantages for the interviewer who simply takes those pos-itive behaviors from life in general into the in-terview process?

Attitude Statements

Comment 20

The interviewer now begins to provide a series of *attitude statements*. Atti-tude statements affect the mood or feelings of the interviewee. By affecting the interviewee's emotions through the application of specific statements, the interviewer works toward meeting the objective of the particular interview. Note the interviewer's use of emotional terminology, and the interviewee's re-sponse, in the following exchange.

I: I can understand that. I know deep down inside that it re-ally, really hurts.

S: I mean, how can you not love something that is a part of you?

[**Note 1:** The use of the second-person pronoun *you*.]

I: That's very true. You have deep feelings for him.

S: Yes, I mean, just because they do some things bad doesn't mean you are going to hate them or hurt them intentionally.

Comment 21

The answer above is profoundly revealing to the interviewer, who would note, among other things, the interviewee's reference to her son with the pro-noun *they*. Compared to *I*, *they* is the most distant, the most remote, of all the pronouns. Psychologically, this interviewee has distanced herself from her son as far as possible. Also, we identify the pronoun *you*, with which she refers to herself. Last, we recognize the adverb *intentionally*, modifying the verb *to hurt*. The interviewer has now learned there are circumstances *under which she would hurt the child*—not *intentionally, but accidentally.* What the interviewer might have wanted to say was: "Just because he did some bad things doesn't mean that I would hate him or hurt him." Psychologically, however, she couldn't answer in that manner. The pronouns and the modifier used in response to the interviewer's secondary assertion add much to what the interviewer knows.

> I: That's true. Right.
>
> S: I was disciplining him, for something he did wrong.
>
> I: I can't blame you for that. You know, I would do the same thing. I would discipline him the same way. You know, I believe in discipline and I believe that you believe in it, don't you?
>
> S: Uh huh. I do.
>
> I: Children should be disciplined, yes ma'am. I believe that. Okay, so after you gave him a spanking, what happened after that?

Application Question 11: Most likely there have been times in your past wherein you have genuinely sympathized or empathized with someone. When you did so what was your nonverbal behavior? How did you feel? What did you say? Can you interject that same demeanor from one set of personal circumstance into the interview?

Additional Secondary Question

Comment 22

This concluding type of secondary question—"Okay, so after you gave him a spanking, what happened after that?"—is referred to as a *summary return.* A summary return question serves as a summarization of what the interviewee has already stated in the narrative and to direct the interview forward. In this case, the interviewer's question will elicit confirmation from the interviewee that she struck the child. The degree of severity with which she did so still has to be established. However, by answering this question, the interviewee will at least have admitted to striking the child—both to the interviewer and to herself.

> S: Well, I just finished my glass of soda or whatever it was that I had, and I went off to bed. No, Curtis and I were up. We were just talking for a little while. And we drifted off to bed. I shut Jason's door. You know, he wasn't crying really anymore.

I: So Curtis stayed with you that night?

S: Yes, Curtis stayed the night. And I heard nothing more from Jason the rest of the night.

I: So, what happened the next morning? What time did you get up the following morning?

S: Well, I stirred about seven because that's the time that Curtis left, you know, to go to his job. See, actually, I think he was going to just leave my place and go to his place to freshen up. He didn't have to be to work until about nine. But he left at seven. I didn't really get up out of the bed until about … oh, about a quarter 'til or ten 'til eight. And I immediately went to the kitchen and made some coffee. And started cleaning up the mess that Jason had made. Because Curtis wasn't going to do it. I mean, it wasn't his house. It wasn't his child. He didn't feel he had to clean up the mess. You know, I wished he did. But, you know, I can understand why he didn't. Maybe it was just to leave it as proof to me that this is what happened.

Comment 23

In this excerpt, the interviewee has provided a great deal of information for consideration. Much of what she has disclosed emerged as an aside. She has even commented on her own narrative. When she begins to share her feelings about Curtis, the mess, and what she wished he had done, she is giving the interviewer deeper insights into her motivation—conscious and unconscious.

The Interviewing Sequence

We owe the strategy of dividing the interview into two primary stages to Socrates. In his inquiry and persuasion dialogues with students and others with whom he interacted, he used both the *induction sequence,* which starts with details and goes on to form generalizations, and the *deduction sequence,* which starts with generalities and goes on to focus on specific details. How can we relate these stages to the investigative inquiry?

In one case, the interviewer may be interviewing a person who is highly distraught. The interviewee sits with ankles crossed beneath his chair; his brow is furrowed, his hands clenched, and his elbows are held against his sides. The interviewer might begin with the deduction sequence, asking open-ended questions and allowing the interviewee to guide the dialogue in any direction with which he feels comfortable. Over time, the interviewer will notice the interviewee's feet coming out from under the chair, his elbows relaxing away from his body, and his brow becoming smoother. Now, the interviewer determines, might be the appropriate time to go into some of the details of the matter—move into specifics.

In another case, the interviewee may be in the "willing" chair from the start. The interviewer would begin the interview with the induction sequence, using questions designed for gathering details. After such specific areas have been fully explored, the interviewer would plan to move the interview into general areas for closure.

The maximum effectiveness of these two sequences is achieved by their combination. The interview may start with the deduction sequence and move from the general to the specific, with the interviewer successfully gathering useful information. But then the interviewer may note the interviewee is once again becoming upset, so he or she would initiate the induction sequence and return to those general areas already identified as nonthreatening to the interviewee. After the interviewee has relaxed once more, the interviewer can again move from generalities to details via the deduction sequence.

The process can be diagrammed as follows:

Deduction (general) → (details) → Induction → general → details;
Upset → calm → information gathered → upset → calm → information gathered

The various combinations of questioning strategies and sequences provide the interviewer with a multitude of options. The interviewer's options will multiply again when, later in the text, we turn to discussion of the various persuasion techniques.

Summary

The process of inquiry is an ancient phenomenon. Its successful outcome requires a working knowledge of the various techniques available to the interviewer, as well as their advantages and disadvantages in particular situations. The interviewer must be able to phrase the appropriate questions effectively and apply them skillfully at the appropriate point within the interview. The planning the interviewer is willing to invest, the willingness he or she has to continue to learn the craft, and the application skills developed with thorough, well-digested experience determine whether the interview process consistently proves to be a productive or a frustrating undertaking for that interviewer.

Chapter 4

The Persuasion Process

Rhetoric is the art of leading souls by persuasion.
—Plato

Application Question 1: Have you ever changed someone's mind? Have you ever convinced someone to act in a manner they had not planned? How did you go about changing someone's mind? What did you say or do that brought about the change? Were you nice, or were you assertive? Did you notice anything about the other person's behavior at the point he or she changed his or her mind? On the other hand, have there been times when you attempted to change someone's mind and you failed in the attempt? Why do you think you were successful in one circumstance and not in another? How did you react when you began to see that your efforts were not going to succeed?

The ability to persuade is central to an interviewer dealing with an interviewee in the "unwilling" chair. The interviewer has a twofold challenge with this type of interviewee: moving the interviewee from the "unwilling" to the "willing" chair, and doing so in a manner that is within the guidelines of the organizational written policy on the conduct of interviews, the requirements established by law and local public opinion with regard to interviewing procedures. The interviewer seeking the truth avoids those means of persuasion that both produce a confession by an innocent person and remove the certainty the cooperation was made voluntarily.

As noted previously, the process of persuasion is actually the process of transitioning the interviewee from the "unwilling" chair to the "willing" chair. Within the context of an interview-structured inquiry, persuasion becomes a uniquely personal form of human interaction. Herein we have an interaction between two individuals engaged in roles—the interviewee and the interviewer. Nowhere else and at no other time can two individuals like this come together under exactly this circumstance. Do not limit your thinking to the idea that only the doer of the wrongful deed is going to be resistant or a challenge to interview. Within the conduct of the interview, you can encounter resistance from neutral third parties, targets, and those on the peripheral of the inquiry. Whether you are an auditor, a representative from human resources, an investigator, or a manager conducting an administrative investigation, there will be times when you will encounter resistance, and the need to be able to persuade another will become a necessity.

Each role of the interview participants determines the main objective of the individual playing that role—the guilty, resistant, or guilty knowledge interviewee's objective is to withhold cooperation, whereas the interviewer's role is to gain cooperation. One seeks to reach a goal that is diametrically opposed to the goal of the other. The polarization of opposites—positive and negative—of goals that are mutually exclusive is a complex and profound dynamic within many interview situations. Consequently, the interviewer has a challenge: to replace the interviewee's objective with his or her own objective. There is no doubt the complexities of the process, the total lack of exactly duplicated circumstances and personalities, and the infinite variety of options available to the interviewer all combine to preclude formulas or steps that can and must be followed mechanically. Those who would persuade must develop the necessary abilities, flexibilities, and techniques. They must always be prepared to adjust and adapt. Therein is the essence of the would-be persuader's challenge.

In addressing the persuasion process, we continue to use the interview with Rick and John, conducted by one of the authors in a prison setting. Both men have been arrested, interviewed, and interrogated many times. Do not let your attention become so focused on what they have done criminally that you miss what they have to teach with regard to the interview process and the mindset of the interviewee. As you read, carefully consider what they say. Extrapolate what they have to relate into your own interviewing experience and responsibilities. What Rick and John have learned over the years through experience sitting in the other, often "unwilling" chair, they address here. The aspects of persuasion identified by them will be enlarged on herein, reframed with regard to the interviewer's mindset and in some cases left unaddressed to allow for undirected ruminations. What they tell us we can incorporate to become much better interviewers who find it necessary at times to persuade others to do something they had no intention of doing.

Comment 1

The beginning of an interview is a most critical phase. Your demeanor at the very start will have profound downstream consequences with regard to the outcome of the interview. Consider how we greet one another in a social setting. We:

- establish normal eye contact;
- extend our hand to shake hands;
- open our eyes wider as our eyebrows rise; and
- greet the other by name.

In the interview environment, we address the interviewee in a manner most conducive to our success. We may give the individual a title such as "Mr. Smith," or we may simply refer to him as "Bob." In like manner we may give or take away titles from ourselves. We may be "Ms. Robertson" or we may be "Mary." We may include our position titles such as "Detective" or "Senior Auditor." We use titles to separate, elevate, or lower ourselves socially, and the interview is a social interaction.

Never lose sight of the fact the interviewee is "reading" you. If your own verbal, vocal, and nonverbal communication displays contempt, a judgmental attitude, or a lack of common respect for another human being, the interviewee will perceive it. From that point on, it will more than likely override whatever you say or do, and the outcome will reflect accordingly. However, treating others with courtesy and respect never made an interview worse. Always think, "How would I like to be treated, if I were sitting in the other chair whether I was guilty or not?" This is the mindset of a confident and capable interviewer. It is not a loss of power but an outward manifestation of interviewing knowledge, skill, and ability.

Interviewer:	Would you tell me about yourselves?
Rick:	My name is Rick _____. I'm from _____, Illinois. Currently doing a double life sentence for murder. I was in transit coming from North Carolina. I'm a horse worker by trade, blacksmith. I was traveling down the highway, ran into some people on the highways, a current horse-track runner. They go all across the state working on a horse track. I was out there on the highway. One thing led to another, drinking, partying out there on the side of the highway.

One thing led to the other and there's a couple murders.

Comment 2

A good opening gambit to consider after the introduction is: "Before we get started, would you please tell me about yourself?" "Before we get started" implies the interview has not started (of course it has), so there is no need to put up a guard—we can just relax. Listen carefully as to how the individual describes him- or herself. Note what labels he or she places on him- or herself. If you were to enter into someone's home or workspace, whatever was important to them would be on the wall or table. It could be family pictures, awards, religious symbols, or fraternal emblems. This opening allows the interviewer go enter into the home or workspace of the interviewee's mind. How does the interviewee articulate him- or herself or the circumstances going on in his or life?

Once the interviewee has shared something with you, then you share something about yourself. The reason for this is that people respond to people who respond. All we do or say has one purpose in mind—the successful outcome of the interview.

If the interviewee responds with, "What do you need to know about me for? What's that got to do with anything?," you know you are definitely going to be dealing with a resistant individual. You might as well find it out up front and adjust accordingly. If this is the response from the interviewee just smile and continue with, "Okay, Mike, let's get to the issue at hand. Could you explain to me how your billing procedure works?" Do not let initial resistance become an issue in your mind or throw you off stride. This interviewee has just told you volumes about him- or herself. Use that information as you proceed.

Application Question 2: Go back and reread Rick's description of himself. What has he told you about himself? What has he omitted?

Comment 3

Interviewer: When you knew they were going to question you, you got that knock on the door and it was time to question you, what was going on in your mind?

Rick: What have they got? Where are they from? Are they state representatives or are they the local yokels? My biggest question, to

me, in my mind about them is that they
don't mess with my family.

It is interesting to note the similarity in the mindset of the interviewee and
the interviewer. The interviewer wants to know the facts of the case—Rick
asked "What have they got?" Additionally, the interviewer wants to know as
much as possible about the interviewee—Rick asked "Where are they from?"
Last, the interviewer is required to know herself—Rick stated "My biggest
question, to me ..." You see two goals at opposition in an interview with two
participants with similar mindsets.

Interviewer:	Question your family?
Rick:	Yeah. They don't mess with my family, period. I care about me, I care more about my wife and kids. In that essence what I'm saying is that, if you want to jam me up in the hot spot, third degree and floodlights and all that, fine. Don't mess with my wife and kids.

Comment 4

In the foregoing exchange, Rick has identified one of the interviewer's most
critical tasks: the discovery of what is important to the interviewee. The vast
majority of people feel some element is vital to them—family, job, religion,
reputation, and so on. Because these elements are so important to them, each
person is vulnerable at some point or weak spot. Once this area of vulnerability has been identified, it can be utilized to affect the behavior of the interviewee. Open-ended questions are the most effective for bringing these elements to the surface. Additionally, the interviewer should note what topics
the interviewee alludes to when displaying verbal, vocal, and nonverbal
changes in behavior.

Interviewer:	Well, when they questioned you, did you confess?
Rick:	No.
Interviewer:	You didn't confess. Could there have been anything they could have done that would have caused you to confess? Whether it was pictures, statements ...
Rick:	Yeah.
Interviewer:	What would have caused you to confess?
Rick:	Put the heat on my family.

Comment 5

As we learn from this narrative, the important element for this individual is his family. According to Rick, nothing else would have induced him to confess. However, by his own words he reveals his vulnerability to the possibility of his family being involved in some fashion.

> Interviewer: Put the heat on your family. That would have done it?
>
> Rick: Yeah. Because, I can't see in my own personal point of view, what pressures I can handle, I know my family can't. Because they haven't been down through there before. At this particular time, I wasn't new to the game. I wasn't new to the crime scene. I was an ex-felon, out on parole when this happened. And if they was to push anything towards my wife and kids, I know it would have broke her and would have ruined my kid's train of thought toward towards me.
>
> Application Question 3: Having recognized Rick's vulnerability with regard to his perceived respect in which his family holds him, what options are now available to the interviewer? Even the biggest and most ferocious bull is controlled by a small ring in the nose. It certainly helps to know what is important to the individual to incorporate the most appropriate persuasive approach.

Consider the persuasive responsibilities of a car salesperson. There are four people looking for a car, and they all are looking at the same car. The first person is concerned as to whether he can make the car payments. The second person is concerned with regard to vehicle reliability. The third person is motivated by fuel efficiency. The fourth person is wondering just how good she will look riding in the car. It is vital for the salesperson to determine what it important to the individual and direct the sales presentation accordingly. It would be futile to talk to the first person about gas performance when his concern is whether he can afford the car. The same is true within the interview environment—find out what is important to the individual and adjust the presentation accordingly. There is no one-size-fits-all strategy, and to sit and try one approach after another and another, seeking blindly to find something on which the interviewee will "bite," weakens the credibility of the interviewer as the interview progresses.

John:	My name is John _____. I'm from _____, New York. I'm doing seventy years for an assortment of things. Started out with armed robbery, then I escaped from county jail, down in _____ County. Picked up a kidnapping charge there. When we escaped, I was already on a fugitive warrant out of New York.
Interviewer:	So both of you men have been questioned by law enforcement people for a variety of different issues in a variety of different states.
Both:	Yeah.
Interviewer:	Have you ever noticed any kind of pattern? No matter where you were?
Rick:	Yeah.
Interviewer:	What? What was it?
Rick:	The pattern falls that if they don't have X amount of evidence they know is a probable factor in the crime, they are going to ask you about it. That's up front.

Comment 6

Here the individual is referring to the most commonly used persuasion technique—the *direct approach* or *direct accusation*. In its application and utilization, the direct approach is a double-edged sword. Used appropriately and at the correct juncture within the interview, the direct approach is a valid option. However, for the interviewer to consider this approach as the only option available relegates the interviewer to the status of a "one-trick pony"; if that trick does not work, the interviewing "show" is over. We strongly recommend you never open the interview by accusing the interviewee of wrongdoing. Second, and this is especially true in the private sector, never accuse the interviewee of committing a wrongful act unless there is some probable cause or reasonable grounds to believe that to be the case. Just because someone *could* have committed the act does not in and of itself mean the individual *did* so. The idea of accusing everyone who could possibly have been responsible for a wrongful act is anathema to any gold standard of inquiry and the search for the truth.

Application Question 4: Have you ever found yourself in a situation wherein you were accused of doing something you had not done? How did you react emotionally? Can you remember your physical reactions? What were your thoughts right after the accusations were made? How did you try to convince your accuser otherwise? If your accuser still did not believe you, what were your reactions? How do you think someone who has done nothing wrong would react having been falsely accused of wrongdoing?

Within the conduct of the interview, any accusations should be made at a point well into the interview process. The interviewer should refrain from transitioning into any accusation until after the interviewee has been fully engaged by:

- Using questions which allow the interviewee to respond—tell their story;
- Focusing questions within the areas salient to the inquiry; and
- Comparing the information provided by the interviewee with what information was known prior to the initiation of this interview.

This is the time when the interviewer should be learning—learning more about the interviewee, learning from the changes in the interviewee's behavior as the interview progresses, and comparing what the interviewee is asserting with what the interviewer knew prior to the initiation of the interview.

Once the interviewer has obtained some leverage on which to make the assertion(s), the transition can be initiated from a fact-finding and fact-confirmation phase of the interview to a phase that pointedly deals with the issues revealed and/or confirmed. At this point the transition should be smooth, professional, and nonjudgmental. Becoming bombastic and acrimonious at this purpose serves no productive purpose. You are not tasked with passing judgment on the individual but rather obtaining the truth. Consider transitions such as the following:

- "Jim, what you have told me is not lining up with what other persons that have spoken to have related and I would like to explore those areas with you."
- "Mary, I have information that is contrary to what you have related and I would like for you to help me figure this out."

- "Larry, I have a couple of (documents, reports, etc.) that I am having difficulty reconciling with what you have told me. I want you to help me out with these if you will."

Now the interviewer should systematically bring up the issues one by one. Let each one compound the situation and allow the momentum to build. If there is evidence such as documents, reports, or findings, now is the time place them systematically on the table—literally and figuratively—and into the hands of the interviewee. Note whether the interviewee holds onto and examines the document (or other presentations) trying to figure out in his or her own mind the discrepancy or error someone else has made, or does he or she quickly release what has been handed to him or her without focused examination and pushes them back toward the interviewer or turns it over.

John:	Or try to run a bluff.
Rick:	Right. They're going to run a bluff, telling you, "We've got this, we've got this, we've got this. The only thing we want on this is coming from the department, right? The only thing we want to know is where you got it from." I mean, they're not saying that you've got it. They're not saying that you gave it up. And they're not really saying they do have it. What they're saying, they just want to know where it came from.

The use of deception on the part of the interviewer is always a hot topic. Although we may refer to it as "bluffing," it is what it is—deception on the part of the interviewer. This is usually a last, desperate ploy. Certainly if the interviewee catches the interviewer in a bluff, the chances of a successful outcome to the interview are reduced significantly. Organizational written interview policy, legal guidelines, and local social acceptance—or not—of deception on the part of the "good guys" to obtain the truth vary significantly. It is imperative the interviewer understand explicitly the approved criteria regarding the use of deception within the interview prior to any application. Many consummate interviewers never need to resort to deception to be consistently effective.

John:	You know, speaking of your questioning, like Rick said about his family. The difference there, I noticed this technique. I was pulling stickups and my wife was involved. She was doing, you know, scouting for me.

We ran into some hard times and she offered to go out and make money for me. And I said, "No, I'm not going to do that. I'll do it my own way." When we got there, this one guy was cussing and stuff. And they got me handcuffed. So I got a little snotty and broke on the guy. I told him, I said, "Watch your mouth around my wife." So he pushed me down and everything. I started to come up from the chair. This other said, "Man." He pushed the other guy and said, "Don't be doing that, just go ahead and cool down." And they started to be real nice. And I noticed that was the technique. Because when we got to the police station, they put my wife in another room. And they came into me, and here I been doing time off and on since '57. And most of them know me or know my family in that area. And this one guy comes in. He's a lieutenant or I guess he is, I don't know. And he said, "Look, John, you don't want to get your wife in here. You might as well tell us what's going on." He goes, "You know, you're gonna take her with you. She's gonna get twenty years." And this and that. The pressure they were trying to push down on me at that time was my wife. She had no felony. She'd never been in trouble. Well, from doing time, I know they can't do nothing to her. She's a first offender. Most she's gonna get is probation. So that pressure didn't work.

Comment 7

Admittedly, we only have John's side of the story here, but nevertheless, antagonistic, bombastic, confrontational behavior on the part of the interviewer can produce dire consequences on the outcome of the interview and the interviewer him- or herself.

John: So, while I'm sitting in jail, they come up
                            with some other charges. And they had my
                            co-defendant turn state's evidence. There
                            was two of them that time. So instead of
                            going with a jury trial, which I really could-
                            n't win, this one guy, FBI, said, "Look, you
                            know, you never give us no hard time or
                            nothing. Look, we just want to clean the
                            books." I said, "What kind of deal you mak-
                            ing?" He said, "We'll just go with the one
                            charge and just consolidate the rest of
                            them." That's okay. So I cleaned up the
                            books for them. Because he wasn't trying to
                            bust my chops, and he didn't come after
                            me with this killer attitude or nothing else.

Comment 8

The foregoing narrative vividly illustrates the complexities of the interview-
and-persuasion process. Several elements come into play with regard to what
John has to offer. He recognized the "Mutt and Jeff," or "good guy-bad guy,"
approach. He recognized the pressure the interviewer was bringing to bear on
him by referring to prison time for his wife. Because of what he knew, neither
of these approaches worked with John. Most individuals learn from their experiences, and obviously John had. What was effective in persuading him,
however, was logic and treatment that was of such a nature, as John said, "He
wasn't trying to bust my chops, and he didn't come after me with this killer
attitude or nothing else." "Busting chops" and "killer attitude" may play well
on television, but to the knowledgeable interviewer it is just not conducive to
conducting a successful interview while minimizing the possibility of postinterview problems such as recanting the admission or challenging the way the
admission was obtained.

As John stated, there were now other charges, his co-defendant had turned
state's evidence, he couldn't win acquittal by a jury trial, and he did have an
opportunity to make a deal. When he asked the question, "What kind of deal
you making?" he demonstrated a willingness to resolve the situation logically.
In a real sense, he was asking the ultimate question: "What's in it for me?"

Traditionally, these logical questions have been labeled "buy signs." Such
questions include: "What would happen if I did say that I did it?" "What would
they do to a person who said that they did it?" "I'm not saying that I did it,

but if I did say it, what would happen?" However, there is much more to these buy signs than simply hypothetical questions. An interviewee is indicating he or she is considering moving to the "willing" chair. He or she is asking for additional information on which to base a rational decision.

Consequently, the interviewer would respond with those "logical" grounds for the interviewee's appropriate decision. An individual who is operating from a position of logic and reasoning offers the interviewer an opportunity to persuade by means of a *nonaccusatory approach*. This approach, which simply stated is "It is what it is" or "This is what we have," tends to be more effective with interviewees who recognize the futility of denial, given their circumstances. Additionally, this approach is usually appropriate with victims, witnesses, and others involved in some peripheral manner with an inquiry.

The nonaccusatory approach has, at its center, the interviewee rather than the interviewer. The interviewee is encouraged to respond freely and assume a greater role in directing the dialogue. Ideally, questions from the interviewer are minimized. Those questions of most benefit to this process are open-ended ones, followed by secondary questions or statements. The interviewer is attentive to the interviewee, listens to each word, and reacts in a manner that encourages the interviewee to respond by sharing feelings, thoughts, rationalizations, justifications, and beliefs.

The advantage of the nonaccusatory approach is the interviewer has more opportunities to evaluate the interviewee, including the interviewee's more extended responses. This approach allows the interviewer to observe the interviewee's mannerisms, as well as any changes therein, and the interviewee's emotional state. The interviewer can be alert for indications of evasiveness, hesitation with regard to a topic or specific areas within a topic, and portions of the narrative where details are less forthcoming than usual. The disadvantages of the nonaccusatory approach are that both the content and the directional organization of the interview are relatively undefined (compared to the direct approach), and the process is more time-consuming.

Persuasion techniques most compatible with the nondirective approach are some of the same ones to be considered in the direct approach: expressing confidence in the interviewee's guilt by pointing out the existence of overwhelming evidence (including evidence refuting an alibi) and the futility of denial. The persuasive interviewer needs to have the flexibility and skill to integrate the direct approach with the nondirective approach to form the *combined approach*.

The combined approach uses appropriate components of each of the other two approaches. In this manner, the interviewer can adjust his or her approach as needed to produce the desired behavior on the part of the interviewee.

Interviewer:	Let me ask you this. When you say you cleaned up the books, you're saying you told him everything?
John:	I let him know the crimes I had committed before. Because, at that time, the insurance I had, that's the way they deal up there. There's no con games. It didn't hurt me either way. And it stopped maybe some other guy from getting arrested, charged with a crime that I did.
Interviewer:	When you're in there and they are questioning you, what's going on in your mind? What is it you are thinking about?
John:	How to get out of this. Look now, if you're facing big enough time, that you have nothing to lose—is he going to turn his back? Can I get that gun? When's my best shot to run? A lot depends on the guy. If he's coming out with a hard technique on me, like one of the tough guys, all that does is make things worse. For a young kid, you can scare him. But for a person who's done time, all you're doing is building a little more resentment and more determination to get the hell out of there.

Exercise 6: Read the MacDonald narrative (Appendix B). What approach do you believe would be most appropriate? Why?

Comment 9

Once again, the comments serve to underscore the importance of an interviewer having a plan prior to questioning an interviewee. This is particularly the case when the interviewer is dealing with an interviewee in the "unwilling" chair.

Interviewer:	Were you different the first time you were questioned, as opposed to the fifth or sixth time?
John:	Oh yeah. Sure.
Rick:	Oh yeah.

Interviewer:	Can you tell if he's bluffing, if he's got nothing?
Rick:	I was able to tell. I don't know why. It was just something. I guess it was just a natural thing for me. Like some people got a musical talent. They're born with it. I could see through people. At four years old and up until nine years old, I was being taken in and out to see the psychiatrist. That's when I first started getting my real questioning. What I call questioning, interrogating, whatever. And after a couple years of that, until about seven years old, going on eight, the doctor said I was all right. There wasn't nothing wrong with me. I was just a young kid, growing up, an adolescent. But my old man, my mom, thought sure enough I was crazy, I wasn't right. Because everything they tried to get me to do, I wouldn't do it. I'd do just the opposite. But you got to expect that out of kids, unless you raise them a certain way. But that's just the way I grew up.
John:	I think you can tell when a guy's bluffing too because you're doing the crime. You know what errors you made. There's only two things you can't control—and that's the human element and the unforeseen. And if you're doing it by yourself, there's no human element really involved as far as a crime partner. The unforeseen can be an old woman looking out the window, things like this.
Rick:	Another thing is that if, in fact, there is an arrest made. Even if it is just for suspicion. The first thing that always, since I've been maybe twelve years old. The first thing that always pops into my mind, before any questions were asked about who I am or anything. If I'm guilty or not, don't make

no difference. The first thing that pops into my mind is, what kind of answer can I give this man without giving him nothing at all. That's all I'm thinking about. Regardless of what you ask. I'm always thinking what kind of answer can I give you without giving you nothing anyway. Just to give you something so that I can go on and you can go on. And first thing that's always ever popped in my mind, up to this day—what kind of answer can I give you, to either satisfy you where you say, "This boy, this young man or this guy here is just not going to give us nothing. Go on." It's eluding a question with a question, but it's in answer form.

Interviewer:	But what would you do, answer a question with a question?
Rick:	Yeah. If you was to ask me about my past as far as, maybe, a few months ago. In the past. "Well, where were you on the night of such and such?" "Well, to tell you the truth, you know, the only thing ..." And then you go off into something else. To hell with the question you just asked. Talk about something else, you know, or make a statement to something else.

Application Question 5: Think about what Rick has related in the foregoing with regard to our examination of deception. What is he revealing with regard to the cognition related to deception? What is his first articulated form of deception—"without giving him nothing at all"? How does Rick describe the concept of equivocation? How does he relate the common goal of all deceivers?

Interviewer:	Have you ever gone into a room to be questioned, and when you got ready to go into that door, you said, "I am not going to tell them," and then ended up telling?
Rick:	No.

John:	I've done that as a kid.
Interviewer:	But not as an adult?
John:	No. Because I've learned the ropes since I came along.
Rick:	I've learned, I guess it is just the way, I've always been taught. Even when I was a kid. "What have you done now?" "I don't know." "Where have you been?" "Nowhere." You notice I'm not answering, but I am answering. And that's where it always stuck in my mind to answer. The first thing that ever popped in my mind—how can I give this answer to whoever's questioning me? You know if you can beat your mom and dad, you can beat anybody.
John:	You've got a certain amount of tension. I don't know if you would call it fear. It's maybe the jitters. You're thinking about hitting the joint. What you're leaving out on the street. Like I said, you've got a wife or kids or something. That plays on your mind.

Comment 10

John's assertion, "That plays on your mind" is the key. Always seek to know what is playing on the interviewee's mind and adjust accordingly. It may be you want to shift the blame, rationalize, empathize, minimize the act in relation to other circumstances, and convey that we all make mistakes or we are all human.

Rick:	One of the biggest things is what are you going to think of me as an individual? Or are you getting personal about this? Or are you just doing your job?
Interviewer:	Does the way different people treated you when they were questioning you make a difference?
Rick:	Yep.
John:	Oh yeah. Sure.
Rick:	If an officer has an attitude like this—no matter what you're arrested for or if you've

ever been convicted before. That has nothing to do with what I want to talk to you about now. And then it also has nothing to do about you personally and me personally. That's outside this door, outside this office, or outside this department. But every person has his prejudices. If you didn't dislike crime, you'd never be a police officer. I understand that much and I understand why. Okay, somebody's got to do that job. No matter how dirty it is or how much work it involves. Somebody's got to do that. So be it. But how good can you be at that job? If you don't take it home with you. If you don't take it out to the street with you to the point where it eats at you like a cancer. And you become just as callous or just as obnoxious as maybe the next criminal.

Comment 11

From this excerpt, we learn the attitude and bearing of the interviewer can directly affect the persuasion process. The interviewer should not convey prejudgment of the interviewee. Any prejudices the interviewer has must be suppressed. As he or she interacts with the interviewee, the persuasive interviewer will suppress his or her own emotions to focus on the interviewee and the objective of the interview. To succeed in controlling the interviewee and the direction of the dialogue, the interviewer has to control him- or herself.

The interviewer who sincerely seeks to understand the actions, motivations, and feelings of the interviewee is more likely to succeed than one whose attitude is indifferent or openly hostile. As Henry Wadsworth Longfellow said, "If we could read the secret history of our enemies, we should find in each man's life sorrow and suffering enough to disarm all hostility."

Remember this exchange is not a personal interaction. It is a professional encounter. Do not take the circumstances, the interviewee, or the evasive actions of the interviewee personally. Accept the reality of the interviewee's world as it is to him or her. It does not mean you have to agree with the reality of this world, only that you understand it *is* the reality of his or her world. This is not simply the "right" thing to do; it is the smart response. People do not react positively to an enemy. They do not act on the suggestions of an opponent.

The dilemma shared by all interviewers is if they did not care, they would not be doing what they are doing. It is simply necessary to channel the energy associated with dedication into acceptable, effective approaches. Do not let your own emotions get in your way.

Interviewer:	Do you think that interviewers are prepared when they come in the door?
John:	Oh, sure, sure.
Rick:	To an extent.
John:	They're doing their homework too. It's like in questioning. In '77 they took me to court in _____ for a hostage deal. I've got sixty years already. What can they do to me? And these two guys came in there talking about, "Well, the best thing you can do is cop out because if we have to take you to trial, we're going to get you about sixty more years. You got off lucky. We should have beat your brains out." So I got real uptight. And I told them what they could do. And they didn't like that, so they left the room and this other guy came in and he started talking to me in a different way. Just like this good guy-bad guy-type technique. And the other guy came in. He said, "We want to get your partner here eight years, will you accept ten?" So, I said, "Yeah, okay. I'll go for the ten if you'll give him eight." So—we took a cop-out. I got ten years added on to what I've got and the other guy got eight. But the technique they applied was a hard case-type thing: "You go to trial and we're going to get you sixty."
Interviewer:	Are you saying when you question people that have not been through the system, their approach is one way? But when you are dealing with people that have been around, been through it, the logical way is more appropriate?
Rick:	You've got to come from left field with a pro, if you are a pro. You've got to come

from left field. If you're dealing with a pro—and we're considered pros, because of the convictions—you can't come to us with, "All right, you know you're guilty, sucker. All we want you to do is make it lighter on yourself." That general routine, looking for a cop-out. Forget about all that beginner's stuff and that intermediate questioning. Say, "Look, you know and I know you did it." Run it down the way it is brought to you. The way you've got it on paper. Not the way you want it on paper. And you're going to get a more honest response. You might not always get a cop-out. But you're going to get a more honest response if you come to the man as a man. He's going to give you your dues if you give him his dues.

Comment 12

The interviewer must always structure the approach to the interviewee and the circumstances at hand. Interviewers typically have no authority to make promises. This is a critical area mandating the interviewer's thorough knowledge of jurisdictional and organizational guidelines.

Interviewer:	Does fear work for the officer or against the officer?
Rick:	Fear of this one individual if its his first offense, and he is younger. And he's over here in this tank with me. I'm an ex-pro. I know what he's in here for. I know he ain't never seen no hard time. He's young and he's alone and he's scared to death of being where I've been. Not having in his own mind, in his own experience, what he's up against.
Interviewer:	Well, let's say that I was up here. And I was going to be here for maybe five or six years. Would you tell me, or is there a sharing of information here?

Rick:	That's exactly what's done. For the simple reason that they don't want to see, all the old cons around the yard, they don't want to see somebody put themselves in a greater jeopardy than they are already in. When you do get time—when you do get a conviction, you'll learn by your mistakes. That's what you're supposed to learn by your mistakes. Like the old saying goes—when you go to prison, you're not going to do time, you're going to learn how to not do time. It's a college here.
Interviewer:	What kind of reaction should I look for?
John:	You can watch the expression on his face. If you see that there is a weak point, that's good. If an interviewer comes at the guy with a kind of mellow technique—"Look, man, you're facing a murder charge. There is nothing I can do for you, you're going to court. But, why make it harder on yourself?" Lay the facts out, and he may go along and cop out. And again he may stick with his story and just go to trial.
Interviewer:	Based on your collective experience, what questioning advice would you have for interviewers?
John:	Look at the individual you are dealing with. Feel him out first. Find out if he's a hard core or a rookie—new kid. If he goes at you with a scared attitude, that tells you which way you can move on him. If he's coming at you in a hard case, there's not much you can do with a guy like that. Unless you feed him the actual facts. Give him the lowdown—"Well, I've got this on you. You can fight, go to court, but this is what you are facing. Maybe if you take a cop-out, this will happen." Or, "We just want to clean the books." Like in some states they do this. It is an individual thing. If the guy

is *a* hard core, there's not really too much you're going to do with that guy. But for first offenders, the reaction is—look at the person you are dealing with. See how he is dealing with you. If he's scared, ten to one, you can open him up. Find out what are his weak spots or his Achilles heel. If it is his family, he doesn't want them down at the jail, wives, whatever. If he's a pillar of the community, the embarrassing factor, he doesn't want to be spotlighted. A guy like a preacher, and he's been in the community twenty years. He doesn't want to have to face people. If you're going to deal, like in interrogation, if you are dealing with a person, first of all, I think the person doing it has to have some knowledge of communicating with people. You've got to be a good listener. Because the guy you're dealing with, depending on the type of crime it is, if he is a child molester, rapist, or whatever—if you can sit down and talk to him like we are talking here, get the guy to be comfortable, relax. I'm not saying he is going to trust you, but there's ten to one he's got a problem. The average guy coming into the penitentiary has got a problem. He's doing a crime—not so much for the ... I mean, money is one aspect. But other than the guy who's just out after money, there's usually a reason he's involved in crime. He's got a dope habit, he's trying to get back at his people, he wants to make his mother feel like she is being punished, or his father or his wife, his brother. Somebody has done something to him. So he's getting back at them. You have got to be a good listener. You've got to try to open the person up. Find out what his problem is. Sometimes you can sit down with a guy and if he feels he can talk to you, he might not give you every little detail of his life, but he wants to talk. He wants somebody who is sympathetic. If you come at him, "Well, I'm gonna bust your head," or "I'm gonna get you twenty years if you don't open up." I think you are putting him on the defensive. You're making him clam up.

Comment 13

As John has revealed, the interviewer must be able to access a variety of persuasive techniques to adequately respond to various interviewees and their particular needs. These various techniques are limited only by the initiative, experience, imagination, and ingenuity of the interviewer.

Exercise 7: Read the transcript of the O. J. Simpson interview (Appendix C). If you were conducting the interview what approach might you have employed?

Some interviewees may be willing to talk, especially after an emotional experience. Others may simply respond to authority. Still others are affected by the interviewer's use of rationalization. Flattery and shifting the guilt can be effective approaches with some interviewees. Finally, and most significantly, many people will respond to an approach based on sincere kindness and understanding. Being nice and simply listening to the interviewee might not always be enough to carry the day, but it will not cause to interview process to deteriorate. The interviewer can best determine which approach will be the most appropriate from observation of the interviewee. Pay attention to indicators of the interviewee's demeanor, such as speech mannerisms, facial expressions, physical movements, excessive perspiration, and other observable indicators. These can vary greatly from interviewee to interviewee. There is no "one-size-fits-all" approach within the interview process.

Interviewer:	When I am talking to that guy, how do I reach him?
Rick:	Another thing you can do is play the reverse role. Because any time you can let a person tell themselves that they're bad, you not only got your conviction, but you've got the door open for them not to just see the insides of themselves but to see just how fucked up they are. Reverse role—you

	are them and they are you. Put the pressure on them, they'll talk to you. Talk to them from left field. Don't come from the pitcher's mound.
Interviewer:	Who should be doing the most talking?

Comment 14

This portion ties in directly with what we have already discovered about power: Power is the ability to persuade the interviewee to respond. Rick's answer to the interviewer's last question is correct. In the majority of cases, the interviewee should be doing the most talking.

Rick:	The one that you're questioning. You haven't got to be an interviewer. You can be a member of the family. You could be his brother, you could be his father, his wife. Reverse role[s]. Make him talk to you.

Comment 15

In his description of playing the reverse role, Rick has alluded to several complex issues in the persuasion process. For example, it is important to be able to think along the same lines as the interviewee: "You are them and they are you." By establishing commonality, the interviewer can structure a face-saving rationalization for the interviewee's motives (actions). Additionally, the reverse role allows the interviewer to become a person of influence to the interviewee—someone who can affect the interviewee's behavior and emotions. Rick has summarized so much by simply saying, "You haven't got to be an interviewer. You can be a member of the family. You could be his brother, you could be his father, his wife."

The interviewer may find the interviewee becomes emotional when reference is made to:

- the sorrow and suffering of the victim or the family of the victim;
- the interviewee's mother, father, or some other member of his or her family;
- the interviewee's childhood;
- the interviewee's early moral or religious training;
- those persons whom the interviewee holds in high esteem;
- those teachers, friends, or others who have helped him or her in the past.

In those instances where the interviewer observes the interviewee's emotional responses to particular areas, the interviewer should strive to intensify those emotions.

John:	You make him think to himself. Like, "Hey, if I was in your place, man, you know, Bill. I don't know what your mom is going to say about this. Or what your friends are going to say. How can we work with this? What shall we do with this? Why did you get into this? Why did you pick on a youth that age?" Try to make him open up. Because once he starts talking, he is not going to stop. Because he is an emotional person. A listener can do more than a questioner.

Comment 16

What John says here fully supports Rick's answer. The ability to listen is an excellent method of persuasion. Using silence as a technique for obtaining a response is effective and reduces the interviewer's challenging task to a process of inquiry and persuasion.

John:	When people feel comfortable with you, automatically they'll talk to you. If you're an interviewer, your personality is your biggest asset. When you're dealing with somebody, that guy is evaluating you. Just like you are evaluating him.

Comment 17

This is correct. The evaluation process works both ways. How an interviewee responds to an interviewer will be based to a large degree on that interviewee's evaluation of the interviewer. The interviewer must always appear to the interviewee, through his or her conduct and attitude, as an individual who is simply seeking the truth. The interviewee should be able to discern an attitude of understanding and sympathy in the interviewer. To convey this impression, the interviewer must always behave with a high degree of self-command, patience, perseverance, and integrity. Likewise, the interviewer's use of language and the degree of respect for the interviewee as a person that he or she demonstrates must be such that the interviewer is always prepared for anything he or she says and does to be made public. The interviewer must ensure public scrutiny will reveal nothing less than his or her professionalism and ability.

John:	When we get a write-up in here, for example. We go before a disciplinary committee—just like a court. We've got our story made up before we go in there. We know we're guilty and we know they're going to find us guilty, no matter what we say. But still, when we walk in there he's got a charge right on paper. And a lot of times it depends on how the guy talks to you. Biggest thing is, here you are going before a board—"This officer says that you've done this." "I didn't do that. I don't know what he's talking about. He's a liar. I was down the hall there with my buddies." See, you're prepared for what is coming. But now if the guy is sitting there and you've got somebody decent on that board, that you've dealt with, you'll open up to him. You'll talk to him man to man.
Interviewer:	Let's take the situation you were talking about. You've got your story. You're going to tell them that you were down the hall with your buddies. You tell them that and the guy on the board looks at you and says, "I don't believe you." He isn't mad, he just tells you that he does not believe you. But let's say that you get written up and you're in there and you really were down the hall with your buddies. And you tell him that. And the guy looks at you and says, "I don't believe you." Is there any difference in the way you feel when you are telling the truth and you are not telling the truth?
Rick:	When you tell the truth and you're getting the same punishment, and that's what it is. The man sits there and says, "I don't believe you, I've done heard that before." And he gives you the same punishment as if you

	did it, you got but one recourse—that's to appeal his decision.
Interviewer:	If you know what you're telling him is not the truth, and he says, "I don't believe you"—what then?
Rick:	You just go on. You've got to finish that role.

Application Question 6: What has Rick revealed about the deceiver when he relates, "You've got to finish that role"? If the deceiver is playing a role, how does that distinguish him or her from the truthful individual? If we normally relate an actor as playing a role, what can we learn from Rick as an actor playing a role as a truthful person?

Interviewer:	If you know what you're telling him is the truth, and then he says, "I don't believe you"—does that bother you more?
John:	Sure. If someone is going to be an interviewer, he is building his own character by how he deals with people. It becomes a pattern with him. If he's jiving a guy all the rime and running games on him, that becomes a pattern with him. And it makes him ineffective. If he is sincere in what he is doing and he's dealing with a guy straight up, that becomes a pattern with him. If he's a good communicator and he can listen to a person, the person will communicate back to him. The average guy, when he gets arrested he's looking for a way out. He's got fears. He's looking at what's going to happen. You're looking for *the weak spot to get him to talk to you.* Each individual, as you sit down, you have to evaluate that person. Find out what kind of person you're dealing with—if he's scared, if he's a hard rock or whatever he *is.* Then make your own decisions, step by step—how do I deal with this guy? How do I make him talk to me? To get a guy to be a more effective interrogator or interviewer, if you're talking to a

person who has an emotional-type crime and he knows he needs help—sometimes asking what kind of help he wants breaks the ice. "I'm here, I'm doing a job. Here's what you are faced with. And you know probably what the outcome is gonna be. What do you want? What can we do for you? What kind of help do you need? Is there somebody you want to talk to?" The more relaxed, the more comfortable you make the person feel, the more response you're going to get from him.

Comment 18

John has provided significant insights for the interviewer who is trying to control the behavior of an interviewee. He says, in effect, that the interviewer has to determine what type of interviewee he or she is confronting: Is this interviewee willing or unwilling? Is the interviewee a career criminal, or someone who is in this situation for the first time? In either case, John advises the interviewer the interviewee is looking for help—certainly help as he defines it. The interviewee's fears must be replaced by reasons or the motivation to cooperate. The interviewee must be brought to a point where he or she believes the to tell the truth, or to cooperate, will be in his or her own best interests.

Rick: The more you approach him in a helpful manner, than in an interrogative manner, the more you might get from the individual. Regardless if he is an old con or not, or a greenhorn. If he's green, he's going to jump on that like a frog on a pile of flies. He will go, "Okay, help me, I need help." And he's going to spill all over you. An old con is going to be skeptical, "What kind of help are you talking about?" There you go again—you're reversing that role. He's gonna talk to you, respond to you, once you come to him with help. "How can I help you? That's what we're here for."

Comment 19

We understand from Rick's response the interviewer must make cooperation tolerable to the interviewee. The interviewee will normally not respond positively to an enemy or an attitude of animosity. Rather, the interviewer who is skilled at reversing that role can enable the interviewee to respond to him or her as if the interviewer were:

- a parent,
- a clergyman,
- a close friend, or
- someone who understands and provides advice.

When an interviewee makes an admission, he or she places his or her fate, and destiny, in the hands of the interviewer. If the interviewer is perceived as someone with integrity and empathy, the chances of gaining the interviewee's cooperation are greatly increased.

John:	The two keys in your role are the words "help" and "hope." Because the help there—everybody wants it—"Hope I don't go to jail, hope I can get the hell out of this." Everybody likes to talk. I don't care how hard core they are or how scared they are. They all like to talk. It might be about his girlfriend, his mom, or his kids. You bring in a guy who's hard core, ninety percent of hard cores still have a soft heart for kids—Achilles heel.
Interviewer:	Does everybody have an Achilles heel?
John:	I think everybody does. Sure.
Rick:	My wife and kids. I got one other person that was involved, could have gone without being involved, but because he loved me as much as I love him, he's just as involved.
John:	But, as for credibility on your account—suppose you come to me and you tell me, "Well, your co-defendant copped out. He's told us everything you've done. Signed a statement." That may work for a new guy. But if you pull that on me, I'm going to tell you, "Oh yeah, let me see the statement.

	Bring him in here and have him tell me to my face." What are you going to do then? If you can't produce what you say, you've killed your credibility. The guy won't trust you. Because I've had that worked on me before and I called his bluff.
Rick:	Nine times out of ten, you're just throwing that old scare up in there. The thing is, if you are messing with an old con or a green-horn, you reverse that role. That's the way you get anything out of anybody. Just reverse that role. Let them talk to you, and you can answer their question with a question. You're not saying nothing, but you are. And you're not asking nothing, but you're getting all the answers.
John:	If the guy is talking to you, and if he is married or he's helping his family, these are touchy points. These are his Achilles heel. And if you bring them up, the guy is going to start talking because it is making him think. And he wants somebody to talk to. He's in a tight spot—he's got to talk to somebody. He ain't got no preacher there or his mom or nobody else. And how the interviewer talks to him determines how well he opens up, or whether he cops an attitude and goes on the defensive. And once he opens up about the things that mean something to him, it opens other areas also.
Rick:	To get what you're looking for is communication. It is all based on communication. It boils down to just one simple factor—communication. If you can communicate to that person, and knowing that person for what he's worth—his Achilles heel. If he's got one, don't dwell on it, hit it one time. That's all it takes, one time. Hit it one time and leave it to him. Push it to him—reverse that role. And there's no way that a

man will not talk to you. And is no way—
I don't care who he is. If he's an old con or
a greenhorn, he's gonna talk to you. You've
got to find that Achilles heel. Not everybody's the same way—mine was my family, my wife and kids and my baby brother.
That's the only Achilles heel I got. You can
do anything you want to me. If you want to
go toe to toe, you can do that. Everybody
has got an Achilles heel.

Application Question 7: What approach do you think would be effective
within the interview process as it applies to Rick?
How should the interviewer carry herself in dealing with Rick? What about John? Would you approach John in the very same way? Would you behave toward John in the same manner in which
you related to Rick? What differences, if any, between Rick and John, do you perceive from reading their comments?

For those readers interested in pursuing the topic of persuasion further, we
recommend *Persuasive Interviewing*, by Don Rabon and Tanya Chapman (Carolina Academic Press, 2008). The series provides a text, participant workbook
and instructor guide.

Summary

Certainly, there are abundant psychological, philosophical, and experien-
tial lessons in what Rick and John have shared with us regarding the interviewer's ability to persuade. The techniques to be applied and the emotional
motivations to be discovered are, in fact, as old as the interactions among people. All people have psychological strengths and weaknesses. The strength of
an individual's values and beliefs may provide the energy by which to move
him or her. The weaknesses of an individual's character may serve to make
him or her cooperate.

The interviewer deals with—and acts in—the theater of life. Although the
interviewer's role may be generally defined, the lines he or she speaks and the
character portrayed to the interviewee will, of necessity, be drawn from an interviewer's individual experience, knowledge, ability, and intuition. Always

remember, however, that throughout the entire drama the main character is the interviewee, not the interviewer.

Chapter 5

Pressure/Motive: Understanding Why People Do What They Do

> *There are in nature neither rewards nor punishment—*
> *there are consequences.*
>
> —Robert G. Ingersoll

Application Question 1: Have you ever given any thought as to why an individual would commit a wrongful act? What do you think is the relationship between the causative factor for the wrongful act itself and the outcome of the interview? Is there any need at all for the interviewer to give thought to the "why" prior to the conduct of the interview?

Now that we have examined the foundational components of the interview process—questioning, detecting deception, and persuasion—let's focus on the dynamics present before the act ever happens. What can we learn from the mindset of someone who has crossed the line from being within the prescribed boundaries of society to finding themselves outside of those same societal, legal, or organizational parameters?

Our rationale for placing this examination at this point in the text is to emphasize an interview is not an isolated event. It is part of a continuum or a flow. During the conduct of the interview, both the interviewer and the interviewee inhabit three separate but fundamentally connected time zones—the past (what happened and why), the present (the conduct of the interview and its subsequent outcome), and the future (what will develop or occur after completion of the interview and as a result of the interview). The postinterview actions can include continuation of the audit or investigation, interviewing someone for the second time, charges being made, personnel actions undertaken, closing the file, and so on. Regarding the strategy for and implementation of the interview itself, the present is influenced by the past and the future is influenced by the present. An interviewer who mistakenly thinks the interview is an isolated, self-contained communication event closes him- or herself off to the valuable information from the past and is not conducting the interview with the future in mind. Each of the three time zones adds value to increasing the probability of a successful outcome.

> **Application Question 2:** What were the circumstances wherein someone's behavior made absolutely no sense at all to you? Did you summarily dismiss the actions of that person as crazy, stupid, misinformed, or dumb? Has anyone ever suggested your own actions, which made perfect sense to you, fell into the same category?

From the genesis of an inquiry and ultimately to the efforts of persuasion runs a common thread—the question "why?" Why do people do what they do? Those personal actions that are acceptable to society—and those that are not—provide the interviewer with a kind of human archaeological site in which to search for the why. The words and phrases used by the interviewee serve as artifacts for understanding the past. Therefore, as always, every word the interviewee says is important.

The *Penguin Dictionary of Psychology* defines *motive* as "a state of arousal that impels an organism to action; a rationalization, justification or excuse that a person gives as the reason for his or her behavior." The word *motive* comes from the Latin *motus,* meaning "moved." Terms we would associate with motive include *willing, choosing, resolving,* and *deciding.*

A cursory review of the events of a day provides many opportunities for the interviewer to ponder the question *why*:

- a bookkeeper for a family-owned business having served for twenty years as an honest and loyal employee begins to embezzle money from the people who provided her with a job;
- the arrest of a man who, after serving an eleven-year sentence for raping a seven-year-old child, had recently been released and then kidnapped and raped an eight-year-old girl;
- a college official was arrested for bank robbery and is a suspect in four other bank robberies;
- nursing home operator confessed to killing a fifty-eight-year-old resident by forcing pieces of doughnut down the victim's throat;
- a woman was charged with arson after she set fire to the house of a romantic rival;
- a sixteen-year-old girl was arrested for the shooting death of her father.

In each of these situations, the overriding question is "why?" Why would someone steal from the people who had provided employment and benefits for twenty years? Why would an individual repeatedly seek to have sex with a child, regardless of the consequences? Why would an individual with an excellent position in a college rob banks? Why would someone force food down the throat of another, more helpless person to the point of death? Why would someone go to such an extreme as setting fire to another's house out of jealousy? Why would a young girl shoot her father to death? Were these acts the results of a process of choosing? What had each perpetrator resolved to accomplish? What factors played a role in each decision? What was it that moved each individual to embezzle, rape, rob, burn, or kill?

As stated, the interviewer who must carry on an inquiry is required to consider the past to determine the motivation for the crime. Herein lies the critical link between the perpetrator's motive(s) and the interviewer's increased opportunities to use an understanding of those motives as a means for persuasion. The why that precipitated the crime may provide the grounds for persuasion—for moving the interviewee from the "unwilling" to the "willing" chair. Interestingly enough, the interviewer in the *present* must link the perpetrator's *past* actions to his or her *future* actions—connecting what the interviewee did (commit a crime) to what (the interviewer hopes) he or she will do (cooperate).

The interviewer's interaction with the interviewee is not a type of counseling, in the usual sense of the word, but a type of inquiring and persuading that must not overstep the boundaries protecting the interviewee's free will. It is true, however, the same techniques used by the psychologist—listening, understanding, accepting, and helping the patient or client identify additional options—are also the working tools of the interviewer.

Let's return and examine a segment of the interview with Rick and John. Here we process the interview through another lens—the "understanding motive/pressure" lens.

Interviewer:	Would you tell me about yourselves?
Rick:	My name is Rick _____. I'm from _____, Illinois. Currently doing a double life sentence for murder. I was in transit coming from North Carolina. I'm a horse worker by trade, blacksmith. I was traveling down the highway, ran into some people on the highways, a current horse-track runner. They go all across the state working on a horse track. I was out there on the highway. One thing led to another, drinking, partying out there on the side of

> the highway. One thing led to the other and there's a couple murders.

Comment 1

Even in Rick's veiled narration of the circumstances, there are, in a very exciting sense, archaeological elements to be picked up and examined by the interviewer. Rick states vaguely, "One thing led to another, drinking, partying out there on the side of the highway." If an interviewer were conducting this interview after the fact, and if the interview was leading toward some kind of case closure, she would have the individual expand on:

- the meaning of "one thing";
- the meaning of "the other";
- the significance of "drinking, partying."

For the present, however, these areas provide a basis for our examination and evaluation of the *why*. The terms provided by Rick are all we have to work with for our examination and evaluation. In this case, certainly, the terms "one thing," "another," "drinking," and "partying" represent a combination of circumstances that, for Rick, led to the deaths of two people.

The interviewer needs to pay strict attention to the terms the interviewee uses because they can serve as keys or introductions to the interviewee and the significant circumstances that comprise the focus of the inquiry. To get the interviewee to expand on those terms, the interviewer could say, for example, "Rick, you said, 'One thing led to the other.' What do you mean?" Or, "Rick, you said, 'There's a couple of murders'; tell me more."

People will sometimes do things out of fear, anger, or frustration. Sometimes what they do serves as a defense mechanism, or it is part of a process of rationalization. The primary emotional and motivational bases for unacceptable acts are hate, fear, love, and the desire for personal gain.

What was the combination for Rick? Was his motive perhaps hate combined with frustration? Did the combination include hate for one and love for another, mixed with the drinking in the context of partying? The complexities are daunting and unique to each set of circumstances. The interviewer must be open to and have an understanding of the motivations of others. An interviewer with these attributes may be able to find his or her way into the past and learn what motivated a particular criminal act—and what might motivate an act of cooperation in the future.

People act as they do primarily because they believe a particular course of action is the best solution to their current circumstances. They believe it is the best thing to do. The act is motivated by an intention. In other words, a person acts as he or she does in the belief the act serves his or her best interests. Simply put, people act out of self-interest. Now, the interesting point is the interviewee's decision-making or motivating process, which results in some action, is influenced, even programmed, by a variety of past circumstances and conditions. These influential variables include any and all of the factors that can act on an individual.

The interviewer cannot afford to limit his or her effectiveness by making value judgments (right/wrong, good/bad) with regard to the interviewee's decision-making process and action. What is critical is to understand the *interviewee's* motivational process, the *interviewee's* rationalization process, and the *interviewee's* thought process for making choices. The interviewer is not, however, required to agree, only to understand.

For the interviewer attempting to carry the case through to completion, Rick's statement, "One thing led to the other and there's a couple murders," provokes a need to know what set of factors and circumstances led to the acts of murder. To know this, we have to know Rick, and to know Rick requires paying attention to every word he says. The interviewer must be curious and must have the patience needed to satisfy this curiosity.

Rick:	At this particular time, I wasn't new to the game. I wasn't new to the crime scene. I was an ex-felon, out on parole when this happened.

Comment 2

Here the speaker's terms provide us with quite a bit of information. For example:

- "the game," which means he frames his actions in terms of a contest;
- "crime scene," which encompasses a broad spectrum of crime in general;
- "ex-felon," indicating a previous conviction for a serious offense;
- "out on parole," meaning released from prison only conditionally; and
- "when this happened," a phrase significantly including the pronoun *this*, which informs the listening interviewer as to what term the interviewee is comfortable using with regard to the issue on the table.

Another look at the interviewee's self-description gives the interviewer greater insight into the world of the subject, as he sees it.

- He was a felon, or a player in "the game."
- He had committed crimes before.
- He had committed crimes before and had been caught.

- He had committed crimes before, had been caught, had served time, and had been released on parole.
- Crime (for him) could be compared to a game, with one crime being a single contest in a broader competition.

John:　　　　　My name is John _____. I'm from _____ New York, I'm doing seventy years for an assortment of things. Started out with armed robbery, then I escaped from _____ County jail, down in _____ County. Picked up a kidnapping charge there. When we escaped, I was already on a fugitive warrant out of New York.

Comment 3

From John we hear such phrases as "an assortment of things," used to describe his crimes as "things" of a multiple number and of different types; "armed robbery," indicating a weapon was used during an act of theft; "kidnapping charge," meaning at least one person was held involuntarily; "I escaped" becomes "we escaped," telling us John did not act alone; and "on a fugitive warrant," indicating at least one "thing" had previously occurred.

In this brief summary, John reveals something of his past. Some of the terms are undefined, but we do learn about part of what constitutes "an assortment of things"—armed robbery, kidnapping, and escape, at the very least. We also learn that John cooperated with at least one other person at some point in his series of activities.

John:　　　　　You know, speaking of your questioning, like Rick said about his family. The difference there, I noticed this technique. I was pulling stickups and my wife was involved. She was doing, you know, scouting for me. We ran into some hard times and she offered to go out and make money for me. And I said, "No, I'm not going to do that. I'll do it my own way."

Comment 4

Now, from the foregoing excerpt , we are starting to learn more about John and about some of his motivations. He informs us, for example, "I was pulling stickups," thus telling us not only what he did but also that he was the main actor. He also states, "My wife was involved," the term *my* indicating a closeness with his wife. Although she was "involved," she played a smaller or secondary role. She was, he relates, "scouting for me." John was the leader, his wife the follower. In "we ran into some hard times," the term "we" tells us the undefined experience of "some hard times" was shared. We also know the stickups occurred prior to the onset of "some hard times." With the statement "she offered to go out and make money for me," the narrative moves on to describe a time of choices, options, and decisions. As John and his wife evaluated their circumstances, they determined there were two options available to them—prostitution and stickups. From their point of view, that constituted a dilemma (from *di*, meaning "two"). To resolve that dilemma, they could choose one option or the other: "And I said, 'No, I'm not going to do that. I'll do it my own way.'" Here, a decision was made. As John considered the two options, his self-interest priorities dictated that stickups were preferable to prostitution. Furthermore, his use of the pronoun *that*, indicating distance from a thing or, in this case, a circumstance, suggests, psychologically, he moved (motive) away from the choice of his wife's prostitution and to his "own way"—stickups.

What still remains to be determined at this point is John's motive for choosing the act of "pulling stickups" initially (prior to "some hard times"). What were his options then, as he saw them?

Rick:	I could see through people. At four years old and up until nine years old, I was being taken in and out to see the psychiatrist. That's when I first started getting my real questioning. What I call questioning, interrogating whatever. And after a couple years of that, until about seven years old, going on eight, the doctor said I was all right. There wasn't nothing wrong with me. I was just a young kid, growing up, an adolescent. But my old man, my mom, thought sure enough I was crazy, I wasn't right. Because everything they tried to get me to do, I wouldn't do it. I'd do just the opposite. But you got to expect that out of kids, unless you raise them a certain way. But that's just the way I grew up.

Comment 5

In this narration, Rick allows us to gain more knowledge of his past. From the statement "at four years old and up until nine years old, I was being taken in and out to see the psychiatrist," we learn that for five years, beginning at the very early age of four, Rick had been professionally evaluated and treated, apparently for some behavioral malady. With his statement "the doctor said I was all right," Rick reports on what the doctor *said*, rather than simply stating, "I was all right."

His parents, according to Rick, thought otherwise: "But my old man, my mom, thought sure enough I was crazy, I wasn't right. Because everything they tried to get me to do, I wouldn't do it. I'd do just the opposite." The conjunction *but* used here means "on the contrary," thus negating everything said previously about his mental addition by the doctor. In his own words, Rick tells us his parents "thought" he "was crazy," and he "wasn't right." *Because*, a conjunction meaning "for the reason that," introduces support for Rick's preceding account of what his parents thought and believed. *Everything* indicates "without exception" and "in totality"; "they tried" indicates an unsuccessful attempt ("I'd do just the opposite").

In Rick's concluding statements, the conjunction *but* reappears and is repeated: "But you got to expect that out of kids, unless you raise them a certain way. But that's just the way I grew up." Rick follows up his account of the doctor's opinion that he was "all right" with a sequence of three *buts* that effectively negate the doctor's diagnosis. Very eloquently, he has revealed, in his mind, the behavior he displayed was inevitable—for a "kid" raised a certain way. Rick provides a description of what will become of "kids" "unless you raise them a certain way," concluding, "But that's just the way I grew up." His meaning is clear: Had he been raised differently, his behavior would have been different, perhaps then and subsequently. There is a wealth of meaning contained in the word *unless*.

John: I think you can tell when a guy's bluffing too because you're doing the crime. You know what errors you made. There's only two things you can't control—and that's the human element and the unforeseen. And if you're doing it by yourself, there's no human element really involved as far as a crime partner. The unforeseen can be an old woman looking out the window, things like this.

Comment 6

In this excerpt from John's interview, we learn you "do" crime, meaning "to bring about; cause; produce." Crime was an event he initiated and caused to occur. John gives no indication of having been forced into the act or being a victim of circumstance. Rather, what he did was exercise an option or make a choice, which required certain actions on his part which he was prepared to "do." Although those actions had been established by society as unlawful, to him they served as solutions.

An additional term used by John worth examining here is *control*. To choose to "do" crime was an effort to maximize those things he could control. With the statement "there's only two things you can't control," he implies that not to choose crime would result in more elements he could not control. With the word *only*, we understand that to John, crime provided more control over his own circumstances.

Combining the pieces of what John has revealed to us so far indicates situations ("hard times") occurred over which he had little or no control. To take control, John's best choice, as he determined it, was to do crime. This option could both maximize his sense of control and possibly reduce or eliminate his "hard times." Given his perception of the choices he had, self-interest priorities dictated his exercising the option to "do" crime, which would provide him with maximum control.

> Rick: I've learned, I guess it is just the way, I've always been taught. Even when I was a kid. "What have you done now?" "I don't know." "Where have you been?" "Nowhere." You notice I'm not answering, but I am answering. And that's where it always stuck in my mind to answer. The first thing that ever popped in my mind—how can I give this answer to whoever's questioning me? You know if you can beat your mom and dad, you can beat anybody.

Comment 7

In these remarks regarding his use of deception to accomplish his ends, Rick says, "I've learned," "I've always been taught," and "even when I was a kid." In other words, he had learned to deceive because he had "always been taught" to deceive, and those lessons began at an early age. His proficiency became such he could pass the most difficult test to detect deception of all: "your mom and dad." Once that level of ability had been attained, it then became possible to "beat anybody." Rick's use of deception was less an end in itself than a means to an end. The technique was an early taught, early learned skill that could be applied in later circumstances to dealing with "anybody."

Rick: If an officer has an attitude like this—no matter what you're arrested for or if you've ever been convicted before. That has nothing to do with what I want to talk to you about now. And then it also has nothing to do about you personally and me personally. That's outside this door, outside this office or outside this department. But every person has his prejudices. If you didn't dislike crime, you'd never be a police officer. I understand that much and I understand why. Okay, somebody's got to do that job. No matter how dirty it is or how much work it involves. Somebody's got to do that. So be it. But how good can you be at that job? If you don't take it home with you. If you don't take it out to the street with you to the point where it eats at you like a cancer. And you become just as callous or just as obnoxious as maybe the next criminal.

Comment 8

Rick has provided more insight into some of the individuals who make a choice of crime. Such people are "callous" and/or "obnoxious." *Callous* means lacking pity, mercy; unfeeling, insensitive. In its older sense, *obnoxious* means "exposed or liable to injury, evil or harm," and "liable to punishment, censurable." Those who choose wrongdoing lack pity and mercy; they are unfeeling. They are also, perhaps, at once exposed to harm yet liable to punishment.

The interviewer has an interesting combination of elements to evaluate and some interesting questions to ponder:

- Did someone opt for crime because he had been at times "exposed or liable to injury"?
- Did that exposure cause him to become merciless, or at least insensitive?

- Yet even after such exposure and the consequently developed lack of pity, is the individual still liable to punishment for his wrongful acts?

The situation could easily be read as a Greek tragedy.

The important point for the interviewer to remember and incorporate into the preinterview preparation is the more he or she knows about the interviewee, the more he or she will understand about the motive for the wrongful act in question. Consequently, to convey that same understanding to the interviewee is to increase significantly the interviewer's chances of motivating (moving) that interviewee from the "unwilling" to the "willing" chair.

Interviewer:	Do you think that investigators are pre pared when they come in the door?
John:	Oh, sure, sure.
Rick:	To an extent.
John:	They're doing their homework too.

Comment 9

John's observation, "they're doing their homework too," provides more elements for consideration and evaluation. The word *too* is an adverb meaning "also," whereas *homework* indicates prior preparation, planning, and advance consideration. John implies, just as the criminal (in many cases) prepares and plans in advance, so does the interviewer. This exchange serves to underscore the theme of *proaction* on the part of the interviewee, not just reaction: Preparations are made, options are evaluated, and planned action is taken.

We learn from these narratives, in a very real sense, that the game of wrongdoing includes a "test." Both kinds of players—interviewers and guilty or guilty knowledge interviewees—do their homework to prepare for the test. The question then becomes: Which player was better prepared for the test? Don't, however, take the game too seriously and warn John and Rick, or you may become just as "callous and obnoxious."

Rick:	You've got to come from left field with a pro, if you are a pro. You've got to come from left field. If you're dealing with a pro—and we're considered pros, because of the convictions—you can't come to us with, "All right, you know you're guilty, sucker. All we want you to do is make it lighter on yourself." That general routine, looking for a cop-out. Forget about all that beginner's stuff and that intermediate ques-

tioning. Say, "Look, you know and I know you did it." Run it down the way it is brought to you. The way you've got it on paper. Not the way you want it on paper. And you're going to get a more honest response. You might not always get a cop-out. But you're going to get a more honest response if you come to the man as a man. He's going to give you your dues if you give him his dues.

Comment 10

Rick here informs us there are levels of "players" on both sides of the field: "beginners," "intermediates," and "professionals." (A professional, of course, is someone who plays the game for money.) Moreover, how the interviewer deals with a interviewee should be determined by the status of that interviewee. According to Rick it is inappropriate, even unprofessional, for an interviewer to use "beginner's stuff" or "intermediate questioning" when dealing with a "professional."

If the interviewer is himself a professional, he will acknowledge the interviewee as one also and act accordingly—give him what's due a fellow pro. Consequently, the interviewee will respond in kind and give the interviewer his due. In this reciprocal relationship, however, there is a conditional term, *if*. The use of the word *if* indicates a cause-and-effect relationship. Rendered as a logic formula, the relationship would be indicated by if—» then. What Rick suggests is *if* the professional "player" is given his due, *then* he will, in turn, given the interviewer his due.

Interviewer: Well, let's say that I was up here. And I was going to be here for maybe five or six years. Would you tell me, or is there a sharing of information here?

Rick: That's exactly what's done. For the simple reason that they don't want to see, all the old cons around the yard, they don't want to see somebody put themselves in a greater jeopardy than they are already in. When you do get time—when you do get a conviction, you'll learn by your mistakes. That's what you're supposed to learn. Like the old saying goes—when you go to prison, you're not going to do time, you're going to learn how to not do time. It's a college here.

Comment 11

From Rick's explanation, we learn prison is the "university of crime." Players who commit errors (make mistakes) in the game are supposed to learn from those mistakes. Subsequently, they should not make those same mistakes again. Additionally, other players will teach them what they themselves have learned firsthand and from others. "It's a college here," he tells us; in the prison environment, there are those who teach and those who learn. The purpose of these lessons is to improve the performance and minimize future losses.

As Rick so aptly states, "You're going [to prison] to learn how to not do time." It isn't, however, a matter of going to prison to learn to exercise options other than doing crime, but rather, a matter of exercising those same options with a greater degree of proficiency.

Interviewer:	Based on your collective experience, what questioning advice would you have for investigators?
John:	You've got to be a good listener. Because the guy you're dealing with, depending on the type of crime it is, if he is a child molester, rapist or whatever—if you can sit down and talk to him like we are talking here, get the guy to be comfortable, relax. I'm not saying he is going to trust you, but there's ten-to-one he's got a problem. The average guy coming into the penitentiary has got a problem. He's doing a crime—not so much for the ... I mean, money is one aspect. But other than the guy who's just out after money, there's usually a reason he's involved in crime. He's got a dope habit, he's trying to get back at his people, he wants to make his mother feel like she is being punished, or his father, or his wife, his brother. Somebody has done something to him. So he's getting back at them. You

> have got to be a good listener. You've got to
> try to open the person up. Find out what
> his problem is.

Comment 12

The foregoing explanation serves to illustrate the complexities of a person's motives for what he or she does and the importance of the interviewer's effort to determine those motives. Aided by John's insights, we can distinguish two broad categories of people who commit wrongful acts:

1. One type of individual commits crimes because "he's got a problem." The noun *problem* comes from the Latin *problema,* meaning something "thrown or driven." This individual's problem is thrown or driven toward an attempted resolution by means of criminal activity. The criminal's "solution" may or may not be related to money. Money, John states, can be an aspect, but it is not always the only motivation.

There is a "reason" why he is "involved" in wrongdoing. (Remember the term *involved* was previously used by John in reference to the criminal activity of his wife.) Here is a subtle shift in causation: The fact there is a "reason" supports the individual's attempted rationalization for what he did. (Again, it is *not* necessary for the interviewer to *agree* with the rationalization, but only to attempt to *understand* it.) This rationalization process enables the individual to find excuses or justifications for his actions. In his own view, he is "driven" to crime rather than being the "driver," or agent, of his own destiny. Such a passive role means he is only "involved" in crime, as opposed to being a "criminal." The actual causative factors can vary from individual to individual. One may be a victim of the demands of "dope," whereas another is "trying to get back at his people"—"to punish" his mother, father, wife, or brother. Whoever may be to blame, the individual feels he has been wronged and is "getting back at them." Whatever the reason may be, the interviewer's success will depend on the ability "to open the person up. Find out what his problem is." By determining how and by whom or what the interviewee was "wronged," the interviewer can understand and use that rationalization, including the energy it generates. The interviewer who can identify the interviewee's rationalization process, as well as convey an understanding of it, will significantly increase the chances of moving the interviewee from the "unwilling" to the "willing" chair.

2. The second type of individual commits crimes "just" for the "money." He has made a choice. Based on his circumstances, as he perceived them, this was the best option for obtaining money. Some people choose to obtain money through training or education, which leads to better-paying jobs; others earn it by honest labor; and some, by way of wrongdoing, take the money away from others. In each case, choices were made, some of which were socially acceptable and some of which were not.

For the interviewer dealing with an interviewee from this professional, money-oriented category, it is once again wise to *understand* the motive. That individual made a choice: He chose to be a "player" in the "game" of criminal activity. Why he perceived his options to be so limited is interesting to ponder. Why, for example, did John believe he had only two choices: prostitution by his wife or robbery by himself?

Interviewer:	If you know what you're telling him is not the truth, and he says, "I don't believe you"—what then?
Rick:	You just go on. You've got to finish that role.

Comment 13

Here we have the most interesting statements yet. There is a finality to the sentence, "You've got to finish that role." A role is both a part an individual "plays" and the duties of an office an individual assumes. When we are told, "You've got to finish that role," we are told, by implication, "You've got no choice." The circumstances of that "role" must proceed to the "finish."

We also learn "you just go on." Interestingly enough, this is applicable to the interviewer as well as the interviewee. The interviewer's responsibility is paradoxical. He seeks to know the interviewee's motive in order to get the interviewee's cooperation by means of that knowledge. Yet the true why may never be discovered by the interviewer or admitted—even to himself—by the interviewee. Consequently, what the interviewer actually seeks is a motive acceptable to the interviewee—one that, once again, will psychologically "move" the interviewee. It is ironic, at times, that those who would inquire and persuade must attain a true conclusion by means of a false premise.

Summary

By analyzing the words of two individuals, each of whom has had a life-long association with wrongdoing, we have learned something about the complexities of human motivation. The precursors to any given individual's decision to commit a wrongful act may be sociological or psychological, genetic or chemical. Conceivably, an incalculable number of combinations of those precursors could all, under certain conditions, produce the same end result—a criminal.

The interviewer seeks to understand an interviewee's past actions to influence his or her present or future actions. Therefore, the interviewer must be alert to everything going on—verbal, vocal, and nonverbal—during the conduct of the interview. Though all of these reveal something about the interviewee, one word, one aside, one micro-expression of sorrow that flashes across the interviewee's face may contain the justification, the reason, the motive that "moved" the interviewee to do whatever he or she did. Rarely do such interviewee intentions reveal themselves to an interviewer who portrays that he or she cannot understand or accept.

Chapter 6

The Process of Totality
(Putting It All Together)

As we have determined from our examination of the process of inquiry and persuasion, the various elements—questioning, motive, persuasion, and deception—all come together once the interview begins. These elements are interrelated. Consequently, the various options and possibilities are numerous enough for the interview to take any number of directions and lead to as many conclusions. To assess the process in its totality, the following interview is examined. This interview was conducted as part of a homicide investigation. The interviewee denied having any prior knowledge the murder would occur, claiming he had only asked someone for a ride home and the murder had happened on the way there.

Read the transcript carefully several times. Satisfy yourself you are completely familiar with the interview. Remember that every word is important. The interview is followed by a series of questions about the interview, the interview process, the interviewee, and the interviewee's responses. Ideally, those areas to be highlighted and addressed will have already caught your attention before you read the questions.

I: This is in reference to CR _____, homicide investigation. This is an interview with David _____.

S: Where I met up with Larry was at The Lounge, and I had went down there with another couple, John _____ and Ann, I don't know her last name, his girlfriend. And so I had went down there with them to play some pinball, and so Larry came in, and he played a few games of pinball with us and asked if I'd ride with him to Mike _____'s trailer. Well, I'd known Mike had got married and I hadn't met his wife, so I said sure. I'll ride down there with you. And so, while we were there, I'm not sure how long we were there, they were, quite a bit of arguing going on in the kitchen amongst Mike and his wife and Larry, and then I'm not sure what it was all about.

I: Who is Larry?

S: I don't know his middle name.

I: Okay.

S: Just Larry _____. And so I don't know what all happened there. I just, when we started to leave, I heard Larry tell Mike that he would take care of it. And then we went to Larry's house, and he made a few calls from there, and I wasn't really listening to any of the conversation. He was in the kitchen, and I was in the living room, and went to the bathroom. And since I had rode with John and Ann, and then with Larry, I needed a way home, and so when we got ready to leave, I said, "well, you going to run me on home now?" And he said, "well, I'm supposed to see a boy about some money." He said if you don't mind, just ride with me up there before I take you home, and I said okay.

I: Did he say who he had to see about the money?

S: He never mentioned a name to me. And so, we rode up to right around North Park behind some store there. I couldn't tell you exactly where we were, right in front of the cinema across from it, and sat and waited a little while, and Jerry, as he pulled up, I went to school with him, and knew him when I saw him, but don't, really know him, Jerry _____. And he come pulling up and Larry said, how you doing, and Jerry said, fine, sounded like they was just going to talk. And so I started to light a cigarette, and when I did was when I heard the first shot. And I turned again, and he shot again, and he shot again, and Larry did, he got out of the car and fired through the window.

I: The first time the shot was fired, where was Larry sitting?

S: In the driver's seat of his car.

I: And the two vehicles were pulled side by side?

S: Uh huh.

I: With the driver's side facing each other?

S: Drivers' doors facing each other.

I: Which vehicle arrived at that location first?

S: Larry _____.

I: And how long were you there before Jerry's vehicle pulled in?

S: I couldn't say, maybe five, ten minutes, something like that, it wasn't long.

I: Did you know that Larry had a pistol on him when he pulled in?

S: I hadn't saw it, no.

I: Had he made any statement to you or threat toward this other fellow while you were waiting on him to arrive?

S: No.

I: Okay, what happened next?

S: Okay, and then he got out of the car and fired some more shots through the window and went around the car, went by the trunk, around that way, and opened the passenger door and I saw him reach down for his socks. I assumed he pulled a knife out. I never actually saw it, and he leaned over into the car for a minute and come back to his car back around the front of it, got something out of the back floorboard, I don't know what it was, and poured it over into the car and threw a match on it, and when it started burning, we took off. I told him to get me home, which is what he did. And we got there, and Dan and some girl he was with I'd never saw before was there. And I was talking to them, and Larry left again, I don't know where he went, but he came back a little bit later and fell asleep on the couch there. I was asleep when he came back and didn't lock the door. When I woke up the next morning he was asleep on the couch. And so I got in the car and just went riding around and me and Karen went up to the mountains that day and when I came back, that's when all of you were there and picked me up.

I: Who is Karen?

S: I'm not sure of her last name either. It's Dan's ex-girlfriend. She had come over that night to talk to Dan, and they got into an argument in the house and I had to keep him from hitting her, and it was a pretty hectic night.

I: When you arrived back at your house from North Park, who was at your house?

S: Dan _____ and some girl he'd picked up at a bar, I don't know her name at all, never saw her.

I: About what time of the night was that?

S: I really don't know. I was so nervous about everything I'd saw I didn't look at the clock, so I really couldn't say.

I: Did you talk to Dan then or did Larry talk to Dan at that time?

S: I didn't. Larry went in and mentioned something to Dan about you wouldn't believe, you know, what I just done. And Dan said, "what's that?" And he said, "no, I can't tell you." So Dan asked me, when Larry went into the bathroom, what had happened. I said, "it's best you don't know."

I: You say he pulled up beside the car y'all were in?

S: Right.

I: And you heard the first shot?

S: Uh huh.

I: Then you saw him with the gun?

S: Right in his hand.

I: And he got out of the car then or was he already out of the car?

S: I think he fired two shots, the best I can remember, before he got out of the car and then he got out and fired some through the window.

I: About how many more shots did he fire, do you know?

S: I would say it was a total of four or five. I wasn't really counting them, I was just in shock at the time from what was happening.

I: Then he went around the trunk of the car?

S: Uh huh.

I: And he opened the door?

S: Yeah, the passenger door, front.

I: Then what happened?

S: Well, like I say, I saw him lean down toward his sock and lean over into the car, and so …

I: Could you see what he was doing when he leaned into the car?

S: No, I had no idea. I didn't actually see a knife in his hand, but from what I've heard, I guess that's when he stabbed him, but I didn't actually see that happen.

I: Did you ever see him with the knife?

S: No.

I: Did you get out of the car?

S: No.

I: Stayed in the car?

S: Yeah.

I: Did you see what happened to Jerry after the shots were fired?

S: I just, when I looked over, he was falling over into the seat, and as Larry was getting out, and I didn't really see the bullet on impact, but I did see Larry stand there with the gun in his hand firing through the window.

I: Could you see Jerry then?

S: Not when he fell over in the seat, no.

I: When you say he fell over into the seat, are you talking about the passenger seat?

S: Well, he was driving and fell toward the passenger seat, yeah.

I: Okay. What happened with the gun?

S: I have no idea. I guess he stuck it back in his pocket.

I: How big a gun was it? Could you tell?

S: It looked like it was, I don't know, about like that. I'm not real familiar with handguns at all.

I: But you indicated twelve to fourteen inches long. Do you think it was a pretty large weapon then?

S: Well, it didn't, the only gun I really know anything about would be, say, a Colt forty-five, and it didn't look that long.

I: Did it appear to be about the size of this gun?

S: Yeah, something similar to that, about that length.

I: About the size of a four-inch thirty-eight? That's what this pistol is.

S: It was about that size, the barrel on it, looked to be.

I: How long was you with Larry time-wise before this happened?

S: Well, I'm not sure what time I left with him from the tavern down there. I could ask John or Ann, one of them, they might be more familiar with the time, but I don't have a watch, so I really don't know.

I: You think you were with him as much as three hours? Or four hours?

S: Yeah, I would say so.

I: At least that much time?

S: Uh huh.

I: During that time frame, do you know or do you recall Larry having taken drugs or alcohol or anything like that?

S: Well, he was drinking beer at The Lounge, and when we got to Mike's trailer they were drinking Bacardi rum, had a half-gallon of it, and Larry mixed him a couple drinks of that. I'm sure I saw him do that before all the arguing started. And then when they started arguing, I walked into the living room, and some other couple I'd never laid eyes on before was watching TV, so I just sat there and talked with them.

And every now and then they'd look toward the kitchen and laugh. Boy, they're getting loud in there, aren't they? So I don't know what they were arguing about, wasn't none of my business.

I: Do you have an opinion as to his sobriety or whether he was drunk, intoxicated, or how would you describe his … ?

S: Well, he wasn't staggering and drunk, I wouldn't say that, but I'm sure from what he had drank he had to be high.

I: Did he have any trouble driving or maneuvering the automobile on the way to North Park?

S: Not noticeable, no.

I: Did you see him take any drugs that night?

S: No.

I: None at all?

S: No. If he did, he didn't do it in front of me.

I: When you all left North Park, who drove away?

S: Larry.

I: Larry drove to and from North Park?

S: Uh huh.

I: David, how much had you had to drink on this night?

S: I would say, I don't know, maybe at the most four or five beers at The Lounge and that was all.

I: You didn't drink any of the mixed drinks or … ?

S: No, 'cause I don't ever drink liquor on top of beer, I get sick, and I asked Mike if he had a beer, and he said, look in the fridge, and it was just one, so I said, "well I'm not going to take your last one." So I didn't have anything else to drink from the time I left The Lounge.

I: How about a description of your feelings on your sobriety on that night? Would you describe yourself as intoxicated or …

S: I had a slight buzz, I'd say, when we left The Lounge and as the evening wore on, I sobered up 'cause I didn't drink anything else.

I: Had you been taking any drugs, pills, smoking reefers, or anything like that that night?

S: No.

I: After the incident occurred, did he say anything to you about why this had happened?

S: He really didn't say anything other than, I don't know, he might have mentioned he didn't have to worry about it anymore, or something like that, but I really can't say 'cause I was just in more or less shock and scared myself because if he done that to him and I sat and watched him do it, I was afraid for my life at the time. I was just really not aware of anything.

I: Do you know why he went to that location?

S: No, he told me it was to go see a boy about some money. Now, I don't know if Larry owed it to Jerry or if Jerry owed to Larry or who owed who what, but he said it was about money.

I: Over a debt between the two of them, regardless which way the money was owed?

S: Well, my understanding of it, I couldn't say for sure, but just from the way it looked, it looked like Larry owed Mike, who in turn owed Jerry, and it seemed like Jerry had put pressure on Mike, and Mike was putting pressure on Larry, and so it looked like Larry just went back to the source. I can't say that's exactly the way it happened. I'm just saying that's the way it seems to me.

I: And you say you went back to your house, where you met a lady?

S: Well, I'd been back there and, like I say, Dan was with another girl. Larry got in his car and left. And then Karen came by, and she knocked on the door, and she come in and asked if Dan was there, and I said, yeah, but you don't want to go back there because I knew an argument was going to start between them, and so they argued in the kitchen and argued in the living room and argued in the front yard, and I was doing my best to keep them apart. And so he told, well, he kept telling Karen just to leave or he was going to hit her, and I kept trying to stay in between them. So then he opened the hood of her car and pulled one of the spark plug wires loose, and I told her I would give her a ride home, and they kept arguing, and I said just get in the car and leave. And so I took her home and me and her were together from then on, I'd say three in the morning, three-thirty, something like that, until the next day when y'all picked me up.

I: During the time that you were with her, did you discuss this at all?

S: No.

I: Did you not make the statement to her that Larry had shot a man?

S: Yeah, I did, excuse me, I did say that, but I didn't really go into detail.

I: Where were you when you told her that?

S: Might have been in her trailer or on the way to the mountains, one of the two, I'm not sure. But I did mention that to her.

I: You say you mentioned it to her sometime during the early hours right after you got with her then?

S: Uh huh.

I: From the time that you returned from the mountains until now, have you had any contact with Larry?

S: Nothing other than him. He's called numerous times and said he needed to see me, and I've been scared to see. He said, "just come by and pick me up," said we need to talk, said I'll be walking down the street, and you just pick me up or something, and every time he's called I've put him off and told him the family was there or something like that, or I was on the way to my mother's or something 'cause I hadn't wanted to see him.

I: Why don't you want to see him?

S: Well, 'cause I'm the person that saw what he done. I'm who can fill in the missing link, I guess. I'm just scared of him 'cause if I can sit and watch him shoot somebody else, there's no doubt in my mind he'd shoot me.

I: Did he pour something inside that car?

S: Yes.

I: Where did he get that from?

S: From the back floorboard. I don't know what it was.

I: From the back floorboard of the car you were in?

S: Right, Larry's car.

I: Larry's car. What was it, do you know?

S: I don't know. It looked like it …

I: What was it in?

S: It just looked like an alcohol bottle or something to me. Looked like a plastic bottle about the size of an alcohol bottle.

I: Did he leave the bottle in the car?

S: I think he threw it back in his car.

I: Did he pick up anything off the street or behind the build-
      ings and put into the car to make it burn faster?

S: No, I don't think so. I just …

I: No papers or anything like that?

S: There might have been some in Jerry's car, but I didn't see
      him grab anything from his car. He just started pouring it. I
      believe he had a lighter or a match, one, I'm not even sure
      what he started it with. I just saw him lean over in the back
      seat and pour something, and then I saw a blaze coming up
      next thing I knew.

I: Do you recall seeing him with any small half-book of
      matches that night? Do you know what I'm talking about?

S: Yeah. No, he doesn't smoke, so I really never saw him with
      any matches or lighter, either one.

I: Let's go back to how close the automobiles were pulled to-
      gether down there. You said they were driver-to-driver and
      both drivers had the windows down.

S: Right.

I: Do you think that Larry struck Jerry's car when he opened
      the door to get out of his vehicle?

S: It very well could have hit Jerry's car. I couldn't swear that it
      did. I didn't notice because I was, you know, shocked from
      hearing the shots, but I do know when Larry got back in and
      opened the car, his car door, 'cause he had to close it to go
      around to get back there, it just looked like it was so close, if
      it wasn't hitting it was about close enough to hit. Looked like
      if it had been opened all the way it would have hit.

I: Where did Larry get the flammable material that he, that you
      say he poured into the … ?

S: From the back floorboard behind the driver's seat of his car.

I: If you will, describe the container that it was in, the best you
      can remember.

S: It just looked like a plastic bottle, wasn't, didn't look clear,
      kind of had a white, smokey look to it to where you could-
      n't see its contents and, just from the glimpse I caught as he
      spun around, looked like a rubbing alcohol bottle, what
      comes to mind, trying to picture it in my mind now.

I: And after he got rid of the contents of it and lit the automo-
      bile, what did he do with the container?

S: He put it back in the back floorboard as he was getting in, he just kind of dropped it behind the seat and jumped in and took off.

I: Were you able to smell an odor, like gasoline or anything like that that you are familiar with?

S: No.

I: None at all?

S: Nothing that I can think of. I didn't really notice an odor.

I: When Jerry first pulled in, was there any conversation between Jerry and Larry that you recall?

S: Just very short, and, like I said, it seemed very calm.

I: There was no arguing between them?

S: No. They seemed to be talking calm, like I say, it was pretty much, how you doing and stuff like that, and then as I lit my cigarette I heard the first shot.

I: Do you take any drugs or pills or snort any coke or anything like that, along those lines?

S: I smoke marijuana, not what you would call frequent user. I might smoke one or two joints a week, something like that. As far as pills, I have done a few Valiums before in my life, not much other than that.

I: Were you doing any of these that night?

S: No. The only thing I had had was Budweisers.

I: Where do you get your marijuana when you smoke it normally?

S: From Larry.

I: Is that how you know Larry?

S: Well, I've known him through school, but that's basically been how I've known him the past couple years, something like that. I hardly ever see him, you know, once, twice a week, something like that, and if I needed some, he's who I would get it from. I might see him twice one week and then not see him for two or three weeks.

I: So you are saying Larry is your contact for purchasing drugs?

S: Right.

I: Does he deal in any other drug besides marijuana?

S: He has sold quite a bit of cocaine. He tried to sell it to me quite a few times. But I tried it when I was younger and didn't like it, so just don't seem like it's worth the money to me.

I: David, is there anything else you can think of that you would like to have included in this statement?

S: Nothing I can think of.

I: And you're saying that at no time were you an active participant in the commission of this crime?

S: No.

I: That you were only with him at his request because he was giving you a ride home and asked you to ride and see a fellow that he owed money to?

S: Well, he never said who owed who money. He said, "let's just go see this fellow about some money."

I: A fellow that he was supposed to meet about some money?

S: Yeah, about some money. And I didn't even know where he was going until we got there.

I: And you're saying that you did not know or were not aware of any bad blood between them or had no idea that he intended to do bodily injury to Jerry?

S: Nothing, to look back on his tone of voice when we left Mike's trailer, and he told Mike he was going to take care of it, it seemed like maybe he had thought about it, but no, he never mentioned anything to me about that's what he had planned to do. But after the way things happened and, like I say, look back on it, just the tone of voice he had when he told Mike he'd take care of it, seems like he might have been thinking about it then.

I: Have you ever bought drugs from Mike?

S: No.

I: Do you know if Larry purchased drugs from Mike?

S: Well, he had told me that that's who he was getting some from at one time.

I: Do you know where Mike was getting his drugs?

S: No.

I: Do you have an opinion whether or not Mike knew what was going to take place?

S: I don't know if he did or not, really don't. I wouldn't think that he, that he did, just from hearing the arguing that went on and all, I didn't hear much of it, it was just arguing, and I don't know, he could have. I really couldn't say.

I: Who was arguing?

S: Mike and Larry and Mike's wife.

I: Do you recall what they were arguing about?

S: I just know Mike said something to Larry about money. I couldn't say to quote any price and then Larry said some guy's name, and I couldn't even recall the name. So when he said that, that made Mike's wife just mad as could be and she got right up in Larry's face and was just screaming at him and all, and that's when I walked out of the kitchen and sat down over in the living room area with this other couple and was talking to them, and we were pretty much laughing about it, saying they ought to quiet down so we can hear the TV. Just wasn't really paying a lot of attention to them because I had nothing to do with it. It was no need for me to stand in there and hear what they was arguing about.

I: Do you feel that this covers everything that happened that night while you were with Larry, to the best of your recollection?

S: Yes, sir.

I: You're not leaving out anything intentionally that would remotely incriminate yourself?

S: No.

I: David, before, during, and after the commission of this crime, did you see the weapons that were used?

S: I saw the gun. I didn't actually see the knife.

I: Okay, after you left up there, do you know what he did with the pistol or the knife?

S: To my knowledge, no.

I: You don't know where they are right now?

S: No, like I say …

I: What was Larry wearing that night, do you recall?

S: It was a windbreaker-type jacket.

I: Were the pockets large enough that they would have held a handgun of that size?

S: They were pretty large, like I say, I'm not familiar with guns. It looked about the size of one this officer showed me. I'd say that would have fit in the pocket, yeah.

I: And you didn't see Larry dispose of the weapons anywhere?

S: No.

I: Or have no knowledge of where they were?

S: No.

I: Or whether he kept them?

S: To my knowledge, they were in his possession when we got back to my house and then, as I say, he did leave from there and come back. So where he went and what he done, I don't know.

Examination of the Interview

1. With what statement did the interviewee disclose he did, in fact, know whom Larry was going to meet concerning the money?
2. Identify at least one statement during the interview where the interviewee's use of the pronoun *we* reveals his involvement.
3. Identify one statement in which the interviewee indicates he knew that Larry had a pistol on him.
4. At what point in the interview did the interviewee indicate Larry discussed with him why he had shot Jerry?
5. List two instances involving deception with regard to Larry's gun.
6. With what statement does the interviewee indicate his knowledge of what was said during the conversation between Larry and Mike?
7. Identify two "hidden" admissions of complicity by the interviewee.
8. Identify phrases that point toward deception on the part of the interviewee.
9. The interviewee reveals he expected a wide range of possible types of interactions between Larry and Jerry at their initial meeting. This revelation occurs through the use of one word. Identify that word.
10. At one point the interviewee contradicts his own narrative. What is the contradiction?
11. Explain the extent of the interviewee's drug use, citing quotes.
12. The interviewee uses the phrase "couldn't say" at least four times during the interview. What was occurring at the points where he used this phrase?
13. The interviewee answered thirteen primarily closed-ended questions with a definitive "no". At other points he answered related closed questions differently. What is the significance of those questions in response to which he deviated from the simple answer "no"?
14. At four points in the interview, the interviewee used the term *pretty*. What occurred at those four points?

15.   Recognizing people act out of what they perceive to be their best interests, what possibly caused (motive) the interviewee to participate in the activity occurring prior to the murder?

16.   Why (motive) did the interviewee agree to cooperate (in part) with investigators after the murder?

17.   What is the interviewee's primary concern (motivator) at the point when he is being questioned?

18.   What would have to be accomplished to persuade the interviewee to cooperate fully in the investigation?

19.   If you had been the interviewer questioning the interviewee, what would your strategy have been?

20.   Provide an overall evaluation of the interview listing positive and negative aspects of interviewer performance.

Summary

We have now taken our places in the long historical line of those who have wondered *why* and *how*. We have borrowed the lantern of Diogenes to light our way in our search for the truth. We have benefited greatly from the collective experience of those who lost their freedom yet taught us more about persuasion and human motivation. We have been able to use an ancient source of knowledge, such as the biblical Book of Proverbs, as well as the works of Francis Bacon, and Charles Dickens written centuries ago, in our study of deception.

Just as human motivations have remained the same since humans began to walk the Earth, so have the primary methods by which why can be determined and how can be accomplished. Although the study of inquiry and persuasion has a long tradition, for some of us, it remains fresh, fascinating, and a source of constant challenge. While most people experience some aspects of inquiry and persuasion every day, in all the various circumstances of life, it is the interviewer's unique opportunity to be engaged in a process whose outcome affects the rights, including liberty, of others, a process by which our system of justice is preserved.

Appendix A

Rapport: The Relation to Questioning and Influencing the Outcome of the Interview

In one segment of the interview with Rick and John, Rick shared that he was "always thinking." He went onto say "the first thing that popped into his head (read mind) was ..." Persuasion is all about influencing the thinking that takes place within the mind of the interviewee. Consequently, to the interviewer, how the interviewee takes in and processes information—how the interviewee thinks—is of critical importance.

The interviewee, just like all the rest of us is always thinking. How and what he or she thinks is a function of the information he or she is constantly receiving and processing. Let's examine how that happens and the implications for the interviewer.

Our goal as interviewers is to be able to, through our communication, act on the mind of the interviewee to produce the desired behavior—information sharing, cooperation, and so on. The amazing thing is, for the most part, we can only operate that mind with words. We have to consider, each and every time we speak, how to act on the interviewee to produce the desired results.

As we give consideration to the concept of operating the mind of the interviewee, let's use a more appropriate term; instead of *operate*, let's use *manipulate*. *Manipulate* is a word that tends to gain attention. Some of us may not like to think of ourselves as manipulators. Let's consider a definition of *manipulate*: "The artful control or management of." To "control artfully" to obtain a desired behavior—movement from the "unwilling" to the "willing" chair—is the stated goal of the interviewer.

The point could well be made that to influence others to do something they originally had no intention of doing is nothing if not manipulation. This persuasive behavior can occur in circumstances in which the interview-related manipulation is for the good of the individual—a fraud victim who is embarrassed to discuss the details, for example—but also in the case of an individual who is going to suffer adverse consequences for cooperating. In either case, we must be able to develop, follow, and at times modify a procedure or process. Think of it this way: Someone is going to log onto their computer. To do so, he or she must have his or her exact username and password. Should he or she deviate in any way from the exact combination of either, he or she will not be allowed access to the computer. The outcome would be the same—blocked! To produce a specific behavior from the computer—access—the operator must use the correct username and password. If the username-password process is followed correctly, then the behavior of the computer—the desired outcome—would be to allow access. Once we see this is true of a relatively sophisticated desktop computer, we can readily recognize the consequences of procedures or processes in any operation of the human mind.

The Operation of the Human Brain

If we consider the process by which we operate, and thus obtain data or an appropriate behavior from the interviewee, we have to start with the manner in which information is entered into the mind of the interviewee in the first place.

Application Question 1: How does information get into the human mind? How do we learn?

Answers might include: Experience, trial and error, or doing things.

All this is generally true, but to be specific, information enters the mind through the senses. It is as if there were five information cables attached to the human brain: sight, hearing, touch, taste, and smell. Information is entered into the brain, and we learn when we see , hear things, touch, taste, or smell things. Everything we know, all the data we have stored, came into our brains through our senses. We are literally creatures of the senses—sentient beings. Consequently, it would seem to follow if we learn through the senses, then perhaps we can be persuaded or operated through those same senses.

The brain takes in information through the five senses. (See Figure 1.)

Channels

1. We *see* something and information is taken into the brain.
2. We *hear* something and information is taken into the brain.
3. We *feel* something and information is taken into the brain.
4. We *taste* something and information is taken into the brain.
5. We *smell* something and information is taken into the brain.

Although we may already know we learn through the senses, we may never have given any thought to the fact we also communicate, or speak to others

Information Intake Channels

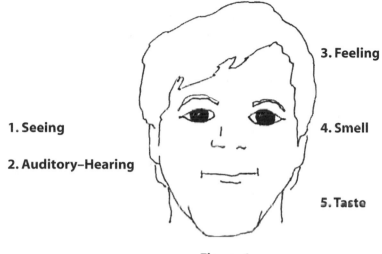

3. Feeling

1. Seeing

4. Smell

2. Auditory–Hearing

5. Taste

Figure 1

(and ourselves), through the language of the senses. For example, sometimes a person with whom we are working will communicate to us through the sense of sight:

- I don't *see* why we are focusing only on the numbers.
- It *looks* to me like you ought to be out there looking for the one who made the transfer.
- I'm just the first guy you *saw*.
- I think you need to *focus* your inquiry somewhere else because if you're *looking* at me, you're *looking* at the wrong guy.
- Why can't you *see* what I'm trying to *show* you?
- What do I have to do, *draw* you a *picture*?

Another subject might communicate to us through the sense of hearing:

- It *sounds* to me like you are trying to *say* that I did it, and I am *telling* you I didn't.
- I have *heard* you have been *talking* to some of the people where I work, but you can just *tune* that out.
- If you think I did it, you are wrong. You're *barking* up the wrong tree.

Still another subject will use the sense of touch or feeling:

- Hey, I *feel* like you guys are trying to *pin* this thing on me.

- Things have been pretty *rough* for me lately, but not so *heavy* that I would do that.
- I think you guys can't get a *handle* on this inquiry, and I came along, so you just *reached* out and *grabbed* me.
- I didn't do it, so you can just get the hell *off my back*.

From this next interviewee, we get words that indicate the sense of taste:

- The whole thing was a *bitter* pill for me to have to *swallow*.
- It left a bad *taste* in my *mouth*.

Finally, we can identify language based on the sense of smell:

- I don't know; he wanted to sell me the stuff, but the deal was kind of *fishy* to me, you know.
- I thought something didn't *smell* right.
- I just thought, this whole thing *stinks*.

Someone may approach you early in the day and ask, "How does that new promotion policy *look* to you?" After that, another individual may ask, "How does that new promotion policy *sound* to you?" Later still, a third person may ask, "How do you *feel* about that new promotion policy?" Each person has made inquiry to you in reference to the same matter; however, each has used one of three different sensory modes.

As you can tell from the above and from your own experience, people communicate in the language of the senses. Each of us (assuming no physical limitations) has access to and can use all of the senses. Our language usage reflects the vocabulary of the senses. However, we usually tend to think in one of three senses: sight, hearing, or feeling. Some people with whom we deal will be more visually oriented, others more hearing or feeling oriented. Consequently, if we are making an effort to establish rapport—to develop that roadway that will carry us together—then we want to be able to communicate in the same sensory language used by the subject.

The situation is the same as when two people attempt to talk on their cell phones. If the person who is placing the call enters the wrong number, then the phone of the second person will not ring. There is no connection. The same analogy holds for people. If the person being called is on the seeing-sense channel—that is their phone number—then for communication (connection) to take place most effectively the other person must dial the appropriate (seeing-sense) number. This would also be the case with an interviewee on the hearing-sense channel or the touch/feeling-sense channel.

Interviewee	↔	Interviewer
seeing	↔	seeing
hearing	↔	hearing
feeling	↔	feeling

We can now determine class participants responding to the question, "How do you get people to cooperate?" were generally correct when they replied: "get on their level"; "speak their language"; "tell them"; "make them feel this is what's best for them." We are simply making specific what we tend to define generally and in a vague manner.

In terms of our rapport-developing strategy, we want to tell the seeing-sense interviewee, "I see what you are showing me and I want to see how this looks to you." To the hearing-sense interviewee, we would say, "I hear what you are saying and I want to determine how this sounds to you." Interviewees oriented to the sense of feeling need the interviewer to say, "I understand your feeling and I would like to determine how this feels to you."

In terms of more personal examples, imagine if you were to be asked about your best friend. Some of you would say, "I like So-and-So because we have a similar *outlook* on things. Our *perspectives* are a lot alike. We see things *eye-to-eye.*" Others would respond, "I like *talking* to So-and-So. We *speak* the same *language*; it is like we are on the same *wavelength.*" Last, some would reply, "I enjoy So-and-So's company a lot. Sometimes we go fishing for hours and will not say three words. But we have always taken the same *positions* on important issues and I feel *close* to him as a friend."

We even use the same sensory expressions to describe those we do not like:

- We never see *eye-to-eye* on anything.
- I just cannot *talk* to her about anything.
- There is something about him that just *rubs me the wrong way.*

If we talk to someone who was once married but now is not, and we ask him or her what happened to the marriage, often the answers come from the sensory vocabulary of touch or physical contact:

- We *broke* up.
- We *drifted* apart.
- We *split* up.

We all use the language of the senses. Consequently, as we work to develop rapport with an interviewee, it is important that we (1) determine what sensory vocabulary the interviewee is using, and (2) step onto that same roadway, which will carry us to the world of the interviewee.

The following example demonstrates what can happen when the interviewee and interviewer use different sensory vocabularies. The interviewer enters the room. The interviewee states:

> I don't *see* why I'm here. It *seems* to me that you ought to be out there *looking* for the guy who misappropriated the funds. I tried to *show* you what happened, but you just don't want to *see* it. But you had better *focus* your inquiry somewhere else because if you are *looking* at me, then you are *looking* at the wrong guy.

The interviewer answers:

> *Listen* here. I'm going to *tell* you why you are here. I have already *heard* your side of the story, but I'm *telling* you right now that you can just *tune* that out. If you think I'm going to *listen* to that *song*, you're *barking* up the wrong tree. Now pay attention to what I am going to *say*.

In this exchange, the interviewee is communicating in visual language and the interviewer in auditory language. It is going to be difficult for them to "see eye to eye" or "speak the same language." One of them has to be able to adjust to facilitate a dialogue. That is the responsibility of the interviewer. Whatever mode the interviewee may be operating in, the interviewer should have the ability to address that individual in the sensory language presented.

Changing Sensory Operations: Why and How

It also becomes incumbent on the interviewer to be able to shift from one sensory operation to another. It is possible to change systems. In fact, it happens naturally all the time. You hear a certain song, and perhaps that song has certain sight-, sound-, and feeling-related memories connected with it. On hearing that song, you visually remember something you haven't seen in a long time. Maybe there are certain sensations you reexperience, and they are just as real now as they were then. You hear sounds that were once part of your life. Your mind has stored all of this sensory data, and simply hearing the song has brought it all back to you.

But the most important sensory channel to the interviewer is the one the interviewee is currently using. That is the interviewer's starting point on the road to rapport and ultimately, persuasion.

Let's take a situation where a convenience store has been robbed by a man with a shotgun. There were three individuals in the store when it was robbed.

You are interviewing, individually, each of the three, and you ask each witness the same question: "What happened?"

> First interviewee: I have never seen anything like that before in my life. I swear to God that gun looked like a cannon. It looked to me like it was curtains for all of us. I couldn't envision any way that we were going to get out of there alive.

Here the vocabulary of the interviewee—"seen," "looked," and "envision"—indicates we are dealing with a visually oriented person. This interviewee should be able to give the interviewer reliable visual descriptions of clothing, physical characteristics, and so on. He *saw* it all.

> Second interviewee: I tell you what. I have never heard anything like that in my life before. That guy said, "Give me the money or I'll kill you." When I heard him click that shell in the chamber, I told myself, "This is it." It sounded to me like he meant business.

The vocabulary of this next subject—"tell," "heard," "said," "click," "told," and "sounded"—indicates we are dealing with an auditory-oriented person. This interviewee should be able to give the interviewer reliable auditory descriptions. He will remember that before the subject left the store, he called out for Bobby to open the car door. He *heard* everything.

> Third interviewee: I was scared to death. I'm still shaking. I just felt like he was going to kill each of us. Even now, when I think about it, I start to melt. It was terrifying. I felt like I was going to die.

The vocabulary of this last interviewee—"scared," "shaking," "felt," "melt," "terrifying"—indicates we are dealing with a feeling-oriented person. As we have all probably observed in the past, this individual was too scared to see or hear anything.

Three people experienced the same event. One showed it to the interviewer, another one told it, and the third described it in terms of fear. This would work well for the interviewer only if every crime was witnessed by visually and auditory-oriented individuals. But what if the only witness were the third (feeling-oriented) interviewee or the second (auditory-oriented) interviewee? How can we determine what a feeling interviewee or a hearing interviewee saw? Just as our own sensory modes can change, so can the sensory modes of an interviewee.

For example, now think of the human mind as a television set. For illustration's sake, there are three channels on this set—the visual channel, the auditory channel, and the feeling channel. To change channels on this set, we must tune in to the channel at which the TV is already set and then change the channel to the one desired. It is as if we were going to take someone somewhere. To do so, we first have to pick that person up wherever he or she might be, then take him or her to wherever we want that person to be.

We make this transition through the use of vocabulary. To find out what the auditory or hearing interviewee saw, we have to change his or her channel. We pick that interviewee up where he or she is (auditory) and take him or her to our desired location (visual) by asking: "When you heard that shell click into the chamber, what did you see?" Having identified the interviewee's current location and knowing where we wanted him or her to go, we made the transition by changing the sensory channels.

It is important to keep in mind the necessity of the "pick up." We have to repeat, using the interviewee's own sensory language ("When you heard that shell click into the chamber"), whatever he or she had previously told us. It is as if the interviewee has given us his or her location: "I'm at Fourth and Main." Now we must "transport" that interviewee to our preferred location with the last part of our question: "What did you see?" Simply asking this auditory individual what he or she saw will not suffice. It is as if the individual in our earlier illustration were trying to log on to the computer by entering only parts of the username and password.

In the same manner, we would take the interviewee whose channel was set on "feeling" and change it to his or her visual channel. We would ask: "When you felt like you were going to die, what did you see?" Again, we begin the process of changing the channel by tuning in to wherever it is already set. To determine what this interviewee heard, we would ask: "When you felt like you were going to die, what did you hear?" Similarly, we could determine what the visually oriented individual heard by asking: "When you saw that gun that looked like a cannon, what did you hear?"

This same process can also be applied to interviewing victims of violent and/or emotionally loaded crimes. Many times we, as interviewers, have said after interviewing such a victim, "He was so upset that he didn't see or hear anything. He's just too upset to deal with it." Again, we have a tendency to blame the interviewee if the results are not what we want. Perhaps the interviewer could accomplish more by asking: "When you were so frightened and scared, what did you see?" Or, "When you were so frightened and scared, what did you hear?"

Some circumstances may require the interviewer be able to change a visual interviewee into a feeling-oriented one, change an auditory interviewee into another feeling-oriented one, and address an interviewee already set on the feeling channel in such a way as to amplify those feelings and use them to achieve a desired end. Why? Because to move the interviewee from the "unwilling" chair to the "willing" chair, the interviewer has to be able to set the interviewee on the feeling channel.

Let's consider another illustration. Suppose the interviewer is working on an occupational fraud inquiry. In the department there are a number of individuals who work with the person who is the target of the inquiry. In response to the interviewer's inquiry, the first interviewee states: "Yes, I saw that there were some things going on within the department. Some things that looked funny, that just didn't look right to me. But the way I see things is that I mind my own business and other people mind theirs. So I think you had better see somebody else about this."

Here is an obviously visual individual. To enhance the odds of persuading this interviewee to behave more cooperatively, the interviewer should change the interviewee's channel to the one for feelings. The interviewer could ask, for example, "When you saw those things that looked funny to you, those things that just didn't look right, how did that make you feel?" Now, as the interviewer begins to hear the language of feeling, he or she can begin to engage in artful management or control to shift the interviewee from the "unwilling" to the "willing" chair. The interviewer would strive to elicit some such response from the interviewee as, "Well, I just *felt* that whatever was going on was not right. I thought he [the target] was going through some hard times."

Next, the interviewer approaches another co-worker. The interviewee eventually states: "Yes, I heard that some things were going on within the department. There was some talk that didn't sound too good to me. But I have always told myself to mind my own business and to let other people mind theirs. So I don't want to say anything about this. I think you had better talk to someone else about it."

Here is an obviously auditory individual. To set this interviewee on the feeling channel, the interviewer might ask: "When you heard that some things were going on within the department, how did that make you feel?" Again, the interviewer would endeavor to elicit a response similar to that obtained from the visual interviewee when reset on the sensation channel.

One circumstance we would want to guard against would be inadvertently switching a interviewee who was already set on the feeling channel to one of the other, less influential channels. How could this occur? Consider the following scenario.

Interviewee:	I feel like you are trying to pin this thing on me. Right now I'm against the wall. Things have been rough for me lately and I was trying to smooth things out. I wish you would just get the hell off of my back!
Interviewer:	Well, I'll tell you this right now. All I want to do is talk to you for a while. I would like to hear your story, and I want to tell you what I know. [Or] Well, I'll see what I can do for you. But I want to show you just what is going on, and let's see if we can't do something.

Here, the interviewee is speaking in feeling-oriented language, but the interviewer is responding with auditory terminology, in the first case, and with visual terminology in the second. Ideally, the interviewer would reply, "Yes, I know you feel that you have the weight of the world on your shoulders and that there is a lot of pressure on you right now. It must be painfully hard to deal with a situation like this. But what I want to do is give you an opportunity to lighten this load and get some things off of your chest." This response, in turn, will tend to keep the interviewee in the feeling mode and can even serve to enhance the emotional state. Consequently, the interviewer has also enhanced the opportunity to promote the desired behavior.

Observing the Three Different Sensory Channels

Although we can gain insight into the dominant sensory mode of the interviewee by the terminology he or she uses, there will be instances when the terms are neutral. An example would be the interviewee stating, "I believe that the situation was one that he should have thought about more before he acted." This statement contains no terms on which we can readily base a response. How will we determine the best response to this interviewee? From which channel (sight, sound, or feeling) is he or she drawing the data on which the conclusion is based?

The answers can be found in his eyes, those "windows to the soul." There are corresponding eye movements and positions for each of the senses of sight, hearing, and feeling. Therefore, if the interviewee is using a sentence composed of neutral terms, his or her eye movements will give us the information necessary to make an appropriate response. The same would be true of a question asked by the interviewee, such as, "What do you think about the new promotion policy?" We would be able to answer "correctly" by observing the interviewee's eye movement. Such analyses are based on studies of standard patterns of eye movements made by the majority of people. Should you encounter the rare individual whose eye-movement patterns are atypical, this difference will be obvious to you, and you will be able to determine that subject's particular patterns as well as any deviations from them.

Visual Eye Movements

If the interviewee is recovering data stored in his or her visual memory, there is certain eye-movement patterns we can expect to see. Also, we can expect that when those patterns indicate visual processing of information, the vocabulary of the interviewee will be correspondingly visual.

Let's take an example of an inquiry into a case regarding money missing from a bank deposit bag. We are questioning an interviewee whose vocabulary reflects the visual in this matter. We make the following suggestion to the subject: "Bill, let's look back at last Friday, and you show me what happened from the time you go to work until you reported the missing money from the deposit bag." (See Figure 2.)

In response to this question, the visually oriented subject should display one or both of a pair of eye-movement patterns indicate visual memory processing: (1) the eyes moving upward and to the interviewee's left, and (2) the eyes looking straight ahead (see top of Figure 2). As expected, when the interviewee begins to speak, he looks straight ahead and then his eyes move upward and to his left. He says, "Well, let's see. I got there about eight o'clock. The first thing I did was look over the computer sheet regarding the deposits. There are several accounts that I have been keeping my eye on. So I looked at those programs until …"

You have been seeing eye movements of this type all of your life, but you probably have not assigned any meaning to them until now. Maybe you remember asking someone when he or she last went to on vacation, for example, and you remember that person looking up at the ceiling and saying, "Let me *see*, it must have been last June." That information is not written on the ceiling, nor is the ceiling just some place where we park our eyes while we are thinking about something. What happens is the movement of the eyes to that spatial quadrant allows the mind to recover visually stored data. The interviewee is engaged in visual memory processing. He or she is recalling an event from the past by remembering visually what occurred. The eye-movement patterns displayed and the vocabulary used correspond to visual memory processing.

Channel Eye Movements
VISUAL MEMORY:

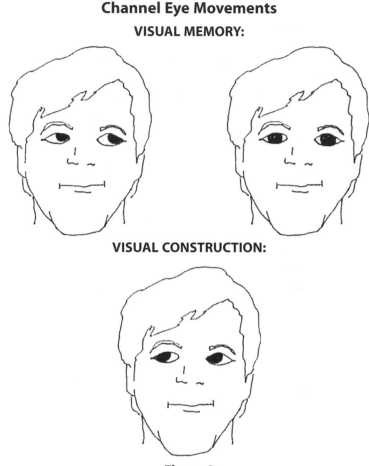

VISUAL CONSTRUCTION:

Figure 2

There is also an eye-movement pattern that indicates the process of visual construction. What is visual construction? Think of it this way: People who work in construction, by definition, have to build. Visual construction is the building of an image. When would visual construction normally occur? One example would be if I were to ask someone the following question: "How would it look to you if four months from now you were given a $4,500 raise and promoted by two positions on the organizational chart?" This raise and promotion haven't happened yet, so there is nothing to remember. What the individual responding has to do instead is to construct (build) the suggested image, evaluate what he or she sees, and then answer the question. The corresponding eye movements for a visually oriented person would most likely be looking upward and then to his right. After a pause, he would probably answer, "That would look okay to me," or, "I would like to see that." Here, because the event has not occurred, it must be constructed.

What about the visual construction of a past event?

Q: Bill, let's look back at last Friday, and you show me what happened from the time that you got to work and the time you notified your supervisor about the missing deposit. *[Eyes shift up and to the left.]*

A: Well, let's see. I got to work about eight in the morning. The first thing that I did was open my drawer to get my deposit bag. I wanted to see *[eyes shift to look straight ahead]* if the deposit and the deposit slip were in my bag. So *[eyes shift up and to the right]*. And ... uh ... let's see ... uh, I saw that the deposit bag was $2,500 short ...

Here is a significant amount of information for the interviewer to consider.

First, we notice there is some degree of visual memory processing and the interviewee's vocabulary corresponds to his eye movements. Second, we notice that visual construction by the interviewee begins to occur when he describes what happened after he opened the deposit bag. We would therefore have to consider why the interviewee was visually constructing while presenting a past event, especially if the eye-movement pattern associated with construction marks a change—that is, if we haven't seen this pattern before with this interviewee. Prior to this point, when we asked the interviewee a question, we would get memory processing and then an answer. Now we have a sequence of memory processing, construction, and then answer. The interviewee is indicating he wishes to look at his response first before showing it to the interviewer. If it looks all right to him, then the interviewer can see it. If not, then the response will have to be modified.

The third thing we notice is a related change in the interviewee's speech pattern. He begins to employ "false sounds": "uh ... let's see ... uh." Again, the operative word here is *change*. Prior to this time, the interviewee has spoken fluently, each word following closely on the last. His speech pattern has been smooth. But once we get past the events leading up to the discovery of the missing money, in conjunction with the signs of visual construction, we begin to get sounds and "empty" words. The false sounds, or hesitation patterns, are similar to the music heard over the phone when someone puts you on hold. Here the interviewee is in a sense saying, "I'm not ready to give you an answer yet, but I will give you some 'music' so you will stay on the line." In other words, "please stand by."

The fourth thing we notice is the number of qualifiers in the interviewee's vocabulary. A qualifier can be defined as a word that modifies or limits the meaning. For example, the interviewee tells us, "That's about it." If "that" is "about it," what does "it" mean? What "it" means is that "that" is not *all* of it. We have to pay attention to every word the interviewee says. Every word is important. Often, rationalization and lack of commitment are revealed through these examples.

Qualifiers indicate to us that the interviewee is having difficulty committing to his own narrative. If the interviewee himself is not committed to the narrative, then we are certainly not going to take it at face value. For example, a concerned parent's teenage daughter comes in from an evening out on the town. The parent asks, "What did you do this evening?" The daughter replies, "Mostly, we rode around." This response would indicate there was at least one other activity beyond riding around. It could very well be the most interesting portion of the evening was not the riding around. The young woman's use of the qualifier *mostly* indicates that not all of the evening's activities were included in her response.

The interviewee has now "looked" at the narrative and has found what he is going to share with the interviewer. He has "seen" something in the narrative, however, he elects not to share it. Consequently, he performs "surgery" on reality: He removes or modifies something. This surgery on reality can be performed quickly, but not as quickly as processing a simple memory. Furthermore, when surgery has been performed on reality, it can leave scars. These scars are often manifested by qualifiers. For example, a former elected official who had once been convicted of crimes related to his office was contemplating running for reelection. At a press conference he said, "The things I did, as bad as they were, I did them pretty much in the open. I go in somewhat with clean hands on the hypocrisy thing." If someone did something "pretty much" in the open, then part of what he did was done covertly. If his hands are "somewhat clean," then they are also somewhat dirty. What the individual in this example would have liked to convey was, "What I did, I did in the open, and my hands are clean." It was just not possible for him to say that. Consequently, he unwittingly provided indications he was uncomfortable with his own assertions through his use of qualifiers in making those assertions.

In evaluating the sequence of patterns found in the interview conducted during an inquiry regarding money missing from a deposit bag, we can summarize what we learned as follows. In the interviewee's narration of a past occurrence, the words flowed smoothly and his vocabulary reflected commitment to the story. Once, however, his narration arrived at the point where events occurred specifically regarding the money missing from the deposit bag had to be described, the narration began to demonstrate:

- construction,
- associated changes in speech pattern, and
- qualifiers in vocabulary.

Again, in the interview, every word the interviewee says is important. Each word is the result of that interviewee's mental selection process, providing the interviewer with insights and a basis for examination, evaluation, and the determination of direction by the application of questions into the area in which the changes were noted. It is not possible to say these changes occurred because the individual was deceptive. We can only note at this point the changes did occur and direct additional questions into this area to explore the interviewee's willingness to respond and evaluate the quality and quantity of the information provided to our amplifying questions.

Auditory Eye Movements

Certain eye movements can indicate an interviewee is remembering sounds. (See Figure 3.)

Eye movements for auditory memory are indicated by two separate eye positions. Both eyes down and to the left is one position. Horizontally to the left is the other. When the eyes are placed down and to the left, the subject will refer to what he or she has heard (external sounds remembered). An example would be (eyes down and to the left), "David said that he would be there on Friday night." When the eyes are over parallel to the left, the subject refers to something he or she thought or said (internal sounds remembered). Examples would be (eyes horizontally to the left), "I told David that I would meet him there on Friday," or "I told myself then that the entire situation sounded funny to me." Auditory or hearing *construction* is indicated by the subject's eyes moving parallel to the right. Eye-movement patterns associated with memory processing, of course, would indicate the subject is auditorily recovering an event from the past. He or she "hears" it. The eye-movement patterns associated with auditory construction, however, would indicate the subject is constructing (building) a sound.

In a modification of our earlier example, we might now ask, "How would it *sound* to you if they *told* you that you were going to get a $4,500 pay raise and if they *said* that you would be promoted by two positions?" An auditory individual would construct the sounds associated with the hypothetical situ-

AUDITORY MEMORY:

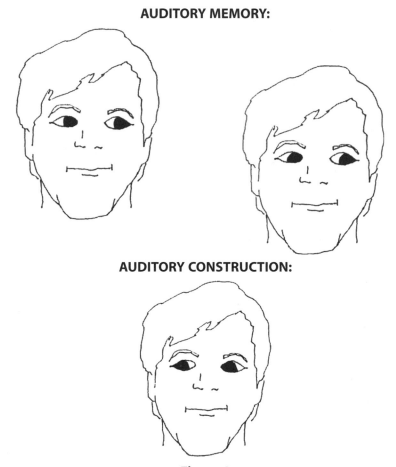

AUDITORY CONSTRUCTION:

Figure 3

ation, listen, evaluate, and then respond, "That would be music to my ears," or, "I like the sound of that," or, "I would like to hear that."

Again, though, if we were interviewing someone about an incident that had occurred in the past and we noticed a change in the interviewee's eye-movement patterns to those indicating auditory construction, we would be alerted. This change would be especially noteworthy if the construction signs occurred in conjunction with an associated change in speech patterns or the introduction of qualifiers into the narrative. We would ask ourselves why the interviewee would now be constructing an event that had supposedly occurred in the past, as well as where in the narrative that change began to show up.

Individuals who are auditory-oriented and who have tried to modify reality can exhibit an interesting characteristic. In responding to questions, they may display a tendency to give answers related to conversations that occurred after the incident about which we are questioning them, as in the following example.

Q: What time did you get to work?

A: As I told my supervisor when she called me to me last night, I got to work around eight in the morning.

Q: What did you do once you got there?

A: Well, it's like I told her. I got there, noticed that the deposit bag was open, and I called the manager on duty.

Here, in both of these responses, we have an illustration of this modification of events. We can diagram the process in this manner:

Actual Event	Initial Conversation	Present Questioning
AE	CI	Q2

As the interviewer questions (Q2) the interviewee about the actual event (AE), the interviewee answers in relation to the initial conversation (CI). He answers a question that was not asked: "What did you tell your supervisor when you called her?" You, as the interviewer, need to shift him away from what he told someone else and require him to address specifically the event in question. He must answer your questions with regard to (AE), not (CI).

Psychologically speaking, the interviewee would rather tell you something true that does not pose a psychological threat to him than something false. It is true this is what he told his supervisor at CI, but we want to determine what is factual in relation to AE. More often than not, this "psychological slippage" is not a conscious process but more of an unconscious attempt to reduce the stress associated with the interviewee's perceived psychological threat—whatever it may be—by offering a convoluted answer that produces less anxiety.

One excellent question that often comes up in class discussion is: wouldn't it be possible for the subject to have gone over his story in his own mind, or could he be auditorily remembering (hearing) having told his story—fabricated though it is—to someone else? The answer, of course, is that anything is possible. Yet in the vast majority of cases, you will still get the construction. The deceptive narrative remains uncharted ground, lacking the landmarks of the truth. There is a compelling need within the interviewee, metaphorically speaking, to stick that foot out (construct) cautiously to test the ground, or ensure the narrative is solid, before walking on it by telling it to the interviewer. This is the same caution that produces associated changes in the interviewee's speech pattern as well as qualifiers in the narrative.

When in doubt, shift the interviewee to the end of the narrative or to somewhere in the middle of it and require him or her to give the narration in reverse order. For the truthful person, this exercise is like running a recording of a football game backward. For the deceptive, however, the challenge is to remember at least three things: (1) what really happened, (2) what they said happened, and (3) the order of what they said happened. Abraham Lincoln expressed this dilemma when he said, "I don't have a good enough memory to lie."

Feeling Eye Movements

Of the three major sensory modes, the feeling channel is perhaps the most interesting. Certainly, it is the most functional for influencing behavior. The feeling channel is "where the rubber meets the road."

How can we discern if the interviewee is already set on or switching to the feeling channel? The answer lies in remembering our own experiences. Let's use, for example, a situation where someone you are close to has lost a loved one. In supporting that person, you have gone to his or her house and accompanied him or her to the funeral home, then to the church and grave site, and finally back to the house. Your friend or relative is sitting in the living room, trying to deal with a difficult, painful situation—the loss of a loved one. As the mourner sits there, burdened by pain and sorrow, and attempting to deal with these feelings, where is that person looking?

He or she is looking *down*. Sorrow, an emotional state, is often displayed by the individual's eyes being cast downward. You probably knew that, but think about this fact: Many times you will start an interview with an interviewee who is initially sitting up in the chair. After working with the person for a period of time, you notice that the interviewee has begun looking down toward the floor. That person has switched to the feeling channel—gut-check and decision-making time. The eye patterns associated with emotion or sensation are:

- Eyes looking downward,
- Eyes looking downward and to the right,
- Eyes closing,
- Eyes fluttering or blinking rapidly.

Experienced interviewers have often noticed these eye-movement patterns before. (See Figure 4.)

You will recall interviewees who began the interview sitting up in their chairs, with their limbs held away from their bodies. After spending some time with these people, you noticed the following sequence of actions occurring with each one: The interviewee's head hangs down, and he looks toward the ground; he takes a deep breath and holds it for a moment; slowly, he exhales;

Feeling

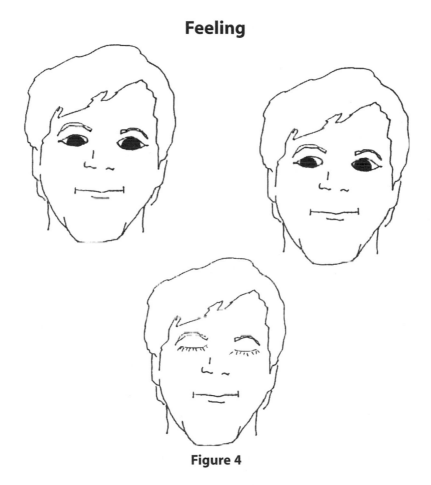

Figure 4

his head comes up, and he may state softly, quietly, something to the effect of, "All right, I took the money."

What has occurred is the interviewee has shifted into the feeling channel. The feeling channel is the decision-making channel. Based on the information he at that time, he makes whatever decision he determines to be in his own best interests. Remember, his most recently acquired information and data came from you, the interviewer. If the interviewee determines it is in his or her own best interest to move from the "unwilling" chair to the "willing" chair, he or she will do so. If he or she continues to believe it is in his or her own best interest to remain in the "unwilling" chair, then that is where he or she will remain.

The challenge for the interviewer is to convince the interviewee it is in his or her own best interest to move. The interviewer can accomplish this if the interviewee is "tuned into" the feeling channel, but that interviewer must be able to read the signals correctly. For instance, when the interviewee switches to the feeling channel (a change you can see occurring along with the change in vocabulary you can hear), and you observe the deep breath sequence, watch for the interviewee's head beginning to come up. If his or her arms and legs continue to be held away from his or her body, the subject will, in all probability, cooperate with you. If, however, the subject exhales and his or her head begins to come up, his or her arms and legs are close into the body at the same time, then cancel Christmas. It is more than likely the interviewee will declare, "I think, before we go any further, I had better get a lawyer."

Once the interviewee has switched into the feeling channel, use the vocabulary of feeling to encourage the subject to stay tuned. Move your chair so you are sitting to the subject's right. A touch on the elbow or shoulder can serve to enhance the feelings of the interviewee, but only do so when appropriate or in line with your agency's written interview policy.

Though there are no distinct eye-movement patterns known to correspond consistently with feeling construction, it is still possible to identify the changes in speech patterns and the introduction of qualifiers into the narrative we addressed in relation to the visually and auditory-oriented interviewees.

Purposefully Establishing Rapport

Now that we can identify the dominant sensory modality of a subject by his or her use of language and eye movements. How can we put this knowledge to use in establishing rapport? If you think about it, you already know the answer.

Once again, let's use the example of your bereaved friend. You have determined, as the mourner sat there, that he or she was looking down. Sitting there with your grieving friend, you wish to convey your willingness to share his or her pain and loss, to be with your friend in this painful situation. How would you sit? Where would you look? You would also be looking down.

Such sympathetic mimicry of another's nonverbal behavior is something we are naturally prone to do when our rapport with that person is deeply felt. We tend to take on the nonverbal behavior of each other. Sometimes we actually strive to appear as much like another as possible, so when he or she looks at us, what is reflected is what we have in common.

Sounds a bit far out, doesn't it? Here is an example: Whenever a (male) police officer is transferred to a vice and narcotics squad, what is the first thing he will do? He will start to grow his hair—both head and facial—and he will begin to dress like those people with whom he will soon be associating.

This process is a naturally occurring and highly effective technique for influencing others. Its tradition as a technique is ancient. In fact, one of the oldest recorded examples of this technique in action comes from the Bible. Paul's epistle to the Corinthians describes how he influenced people so effectively that they converted to Christianity during a time when Christians were severely persecuted. He stated:

> And unto the Jews I became as a Jew, that I might gain the Jews; to them that are under the law, as under the law, that I might gain them that are under the law. To them that are without law, as without law (being not without law to God, but under the law to Christ), that I might gain them that are without law. To the weak became I as weak, that I might gain the weak: I am made all things to all men, that I might by all means save some. (I Corinthians 9:20–22)

The psychological insight here is that to influence another's behavior, you have to enter that person's world. The other person has to recognize some kind of commonality between the two of you, even a reflection of him- or herself in you. The more of themselves others can identify in you, the greater their tendency to be influenced by you.

Consequently, interviewers need to recognize and exploit this psychological phenomenon in interviewing and influencing others. As already discussed, we endeavor to "speak the interviewee's language" by adopting the same sensory figures of speech as those used by the interviewee:

- I see what you are showing me. Look at this for me.
- I hear what you are saying to me. Listen to this.
- I understand how you feel. I want you to get a handle on this.

Additionally, we should adopt the interviewee's nonverbal behavior so, as he or she looks at us, the interviewee sees a reflection of him- or herself.

For example, if the interviewee is sitting in a chair facing the interviewer, the interviewer will adopt a posture similar to the interviewee's. If the interviewee has his right leg crossed over his left, the interviewer will sit with his left leg crossed over his right—just like a reflection in a mirror. If the interviewee has his right hand to his chin, the interviewer will have his left hand to his own chin. Now, your first reaction to this might be, "I would feel stupid trying to do that." The key to becoming comfortable with this technique is to practice it outside of the interviewing context until the process becomes automatic enough to feel natural in more significant situations. For example, practice this technique while watching interview programs on television. By becoming a reflection of the person on the screen, you can improve your technique and practice looking for the telltale eye movements and listening for the appropriate vocabulary.

When conversing with others in situations that are not critical, conscious practice will enhance your skills. Simply watching the process occur naturally among others while they are communicating also helps. During an actual interview, the interviewer would simply put the process on automatic. Just as in learning to perform any skilled task, once someone can do it without thinking, he or she will have achieved an effective level of performance. Once the skill has been internalized, it can be performed automatically. Just as too much conscious attention to such skills can cause clumsiness, if the interviewer attempts to use this technique consciously in critical circumstances, the technique will be too obvious and stilted, thus running the risk of alerting the interviewee to the interviewer's intentions.

Determining the Existence of Rapport

After interacting with the interviewee in this manner for a period of time, the interviewer will want to determine if a rapport has been established. How long the interviewer waits before trying to make this determination depends on his or her ability as well as those subtle variables peculiar to each interviewee. With practice, the interviewer will know when to ascertain the presence of rapport.

One way to test for established rapport is to introduce some change into your own nonverbal behavior: Begin to nod your head slowly, for example, or raise your hand, cross your legs, and so on. If the interviewee begins to reflect your behavior, you have established a rapport. The road between the interviewer and the interviewee has been laid, and the interviewer can now travel that road into the interviewee's world to influence his or her behavior. If the interviewee does not begin to reflect the interviewer's behavior, the interviewer must resume the process of reflecting the interviewee. Often the success of this process is a function of the time invested in it.

In his book *David Copperfield*, Charles Dickens gives an excellent example of how this reflecting process can influence behavior. In this novel, a privileged, handsome young man named Steerforth meets and sets out to charm a constantly complaining old widow named Mrs. Gummidge. Steerforth demonstrates this reflecting process in the following excerpt.

Mrs. Gummidge as usual was taken poorly in her spirits when we showed a disposition to be merry, and was as usual adjured by Mr. Peggotty to cheer up.

"No, Dan'l," said Mrs. Gummidge, shaking her head, "I gets worse and worse. I had far better go in the House tomorrow afore breakfast."

"No, no," cried Steerforth, "don't say so! What's the matter?"

"You don't know me, sir," said the doleful Gummidge, "or you wouldn't ask."

"The loss is mine," said Steerforth coaxingly, "but let us know each other better. What's the matter?"

Mrs. Gummidge shed tears, and stated her unfortunate condition in the usual terms. "I'm a lone lorn creetur', and everything goes contrary with me!"

"No!" cried Steerforth, "why, we must be designed by Heaven for one another. I'm a lone lorn creature myself, and everything has gone contrary with me from my cradle. Mr. Peggotty, will you change places, and allow me to sit next to her?"

The immediate effect of this on Mrs. Gummidge was to make her laugh. "You lone and lorn!" cried Mrs. Gummidge, peevishly. "Yes! Your looks is like it!"

"They are as like it as yours are," said Steerforth, taking his seat beside her.

"Indeed!" said Mrs. Gummidge, with another laugh.

"Ay, indeed!" cried Steerforth. "Come! Let us be lone and lorn together. Everything shall go contrary with us both, and we'll go contrary with all the world."

It was in vain for Mrs. Gummidge to resist this league, or to try to push him away. He sat there all the rest of the evening, and, whenever Mrs. Gummidge began to shake her head, repeated his proposal. The consequence was that Mrs. Gummidge was continually laughing and pushing him, and had so little leisure for being miserable that she said next day she thought she must have been bewitched. (Charles Dickens, *David Copperfield*, London: New American Library, 1962.)

Here the old lady looked at the young man and saw herself. That is precisely what we, as interviewers, want to accomplish. We want the interviewee to look at us and see something of themselves—something on which we can build a rapport.

Influencing through Rapport. Once a rapport has been established, there are several options available to the interviewer for influencing the behavior of an interviewee, whether a suspect, victim, or a witness. The following choices, mundane as they may seem, are nevertheless highly effective. As a matter of fact, it is precisely their lack of appeal that partly contributes to their effectiveness.

Persuading by the Use of a Story

The main goal of a story is to affect the feelings. Consider, for example, the following typical situation. A woman named Mary has a co-worker who she suspects is stealing from the company. She does not know for sure—she only has a strong suspicion. Mary's dilemma is she is concerned for both her friend and the company. She is anxious about the possible consequences for her friend and for her company with regard to her decision to cooperate or not during the interview. The confused subject, like Mary, will tend to remain in the "unwilling" chair.

After establishing a rapport with her, the interviewer can attempt to influence Mary's behavior by using a story. A story is an effective device for influencing another's feelings or actions. The interviewer's story might be offered to Mary in the following way.

> Mary, you remind me of a woman who I was talking with the other day. It was a very similar situation. She was concerned about her associate, as any friend would be. But she was also concerned about her company, just as any loyal employee would be. While we were together, she decided that the best thing to do was to put everything on the table, and so she did. The next day, she called me and said that she really felt good about what she had done because now she realized that she could not get her friend in trouble. Only her friend could do that. But she realized that she could help her friend from getting into trouble any deeper that she possibly already was.

The key elements in this narrative are "she decided" and "she really felt good." This was a decision she had made and had felt good about making. Such feeling-related vocabulary can serve to enhance the story's effectiveness. Often, the interviewer observes the interviewee responding emotionally to the story. For example, the interviewee will often nod slightly, indicating involvement in the story and, in this case, identification with the female character.

The interviewer should be alert, however, because sometimes the interviewee will ask how the story ended: "What happened to that woman's friend?" With the use of a story, the interviewer should always anticipate such questioning and be prepared to offer an appropriate response. Perhaps the interviewer in this example could respond: "You know, many studies have indicated that people who do this were responding to some crisis in their life. It is only by breaking this cycle that we—you and I—can stop this situation from continuing." The interviewer must be especially careful to avoid making any statement that could be misunderstood as promising a specific sanction, particularly where a target of an inquiry is involved.

The use of a story is very common in the persuasion of another. Parents will often say to a child, for example, "Let me tell you about the little boy who would not brush his teeth and what happened to him." The Bible contains many stories used for persuasive effect, such as the parable of the five talents in the Gospel of Matthew (Matthew 24:14–15). A story enables an interviewee to identify with a character in a similar situation, showing that he or she is not the first person to experience the situation and the anxiety, fear, doubt, and other feelings. Others in similar circumstances have shared the experience and have followed certain courses of action.

Any interviewer with any experience at all can draw on a wealth of situations to use as examples. Additionally, the experiences of other interviewers can be recounted to the interviewee. These examples can be drawn from a variety of circumstances and ideas. An additional benefit of using a story is that it can enable an interviewee to admit to an act and save face at the same time. The interviewer's observation of the interviewee can suggest how to adjust a story to fit the interviewee's character. The following story is another example:

> Bill, you remind me of a man that I was talking with the other day. It was a similar situation. He had been a loyal employee of a company for twenty years, just like you. Through no fault of his own—a medical crisis involving his wife—he got behind on his house payment and other payments. The overdue bills kept coming, the bill collectors kept calling and the pressure kept building. Finally he decided to borrow some money from the company just until he could get his wife well again and then he planned to begin putting all of the money he had borrowed back. And I am thinking that something along those same lines is what happened here, didn't it, Bill? You did everything you could to keep your head above the water financially didn't you? Then when you go to the absolute end of your rope you simply planned to borrow the money temporarily, get your wife well again and then pay the money back.

Admittedly, this is a challenging technique for some interviewers to use. As interviewers, we have to remember the goal at this point in the interview is to get the interviewee to admit what he or she did. We want for him or her to tell us that he or she committed the wrongful act. Without the interviewee's admission (willingness), we may never move the process forward.

Once we obtain an admission, we can begin to address the physical evidence or documentation related to the inquiry. The interviewee's admission is the first crack in the wall. If we can then work on that crack, we might enlarge it enough for the entire truth to pass through.

A story can also be appropriate in dealing with a victim, as the following example shows.

> Ann, you remind me of a young girl who was in here with me before. It was a similar situation. What had happened to her was awful, just like with you. She did not want even to think about what had happened to her, much less talk about it. She especially did not want to talk about it to me. But we spent some time together, and she decided that the best thing to do was to share with me everything that she could remember about what had happened, as painful as it was. Later, she called me and said she really felt good about cooperating. She said that if her helping us to help her would prevent this terrible thing from happening to another young girl—prevent another young girl from having to experience this same painful situation—it was worth it.

The use of a story is often an effective addition to the interviewer's selection of options for influencing behavior. An appropriate story, following the establishment of a rapport, may serve to guide the interviewee gently from the "unwilling" to the "willing" chair.

Persuading through the Use of Illustrations. An additional option the interviewer can consider using is an illustration. Through the use of an illustration, a difficult situation can be presented in a more concrete, understandable manner. Illustrations can provide explanation, support a recommendation or suggested course of action, and make a calculated impression on the interviewee's mind.

Often illustrations are phrased as metaphors or similes, in which the words *like* or *as* are found. Again, the Bible contains many illustrations, some brief, others extended as parables. These are intended to inform and motivate, as in this example: "The kingdom of Heaven is like a fig tree." The listener who heard those words would probably have had a difficult time comprehending the kingdom of Heaven but would have been able to recognize a fig tree. In such an illustration, the comparison between something unknown and something familiar suggests a way to apply what one knows and understands to whatever seems new or incomprehensible in the present situation. In the possible internal theft case, for example, the interviewer talking the loyal employee might make the following use of an illustration.

Interviewer:	Mary, it's like this. It's like you were going to put your friend on a boat, and you had a choice. You could put her on a good boat. The boat is sound and new. And on that boat we know that your friend will make it to wherever she needs to go. We'll call that boat the "safe boat." Or you could put her on another boat. This boat has not been taken care of. It is not safe; it leaks, and you can't steer it. If your friend gets on that boat, you don't even know if she will make it or not. We'll call that boat the "dangerous boat." Now, you are her friend, and you've got a choice. You can put her on the safe boat or on the dangerous boat. Which boat would you put her on?
Mary:	I'd put her on the boat that was safe.
Interviewer:	I know you would, but that is what this is like. It's not going to get any better, and it's not going to go away. And you're the only one, Mary, the only one who can put her on the safe boat. And, Mary, it's not possible for her just not to get on either boat because, whichever boat you choose not to put her on, she will automatically get on the other one.

Although the interviewee may have a difficult time recognizing or dealing with her conflicting emotions—concern for her friend and concern for the company—she can understand the image of putting her friend on one of the boats. The illustration of the two boats and its correlation to her situation can be applied to her decision-making process in her present circumstances. An illustration can serve a vital function in terms of influencing the interviewee's feelings.

Persuading through the Use of Suggestion. The power of suggestion can also help move a interviewee from the "unwilling" chair to the "willing" chair. Suggestion involves placing an idea before a person in a way that he or she uncritically accepts the idea as originating from within. An example of the use of suggestion in our inquiry would be the following statement by the interviewer: "Mary, as you sit there in that chair and drink your coffee, you begin to understand that the best thing you can do for your friend, the best thing you can do for your company, is to cooperate in this matter."

Logically, we cannot understand the connection between sitting in a chair, drinking a cup of coffee, and cooperating with the interviewer. What we have to factor in here is the power of rapport, that roadway from one person to another that allows these techniques of persuasion to be effective. In the example, we have suggested a connection between some actual behavior—sitting in a chair and drinking coffee—and the behavior we want to elicit—cooperation.

If the interviewee were spinning her wedding ring around her finger instead, we would use that behavior in the suggestion. Even if the only behavior actually occurring were to be the interviewee sitting there and thinking, we could use that, perhaps saying, "Mary, as you sit there and think about this situation, you begin to understand the best thing you can do for your friend, the best thing you can do for your company, is to cooperate in this matter." Like telling stories and devising illustrations, influencing others by means of suggestion is an everyday occurrence. You have often heard someone say, "You go, and you'll have a good time," or "Sleep on this tonight, and in the morning you'll realize ..."

Stories, illustrations, and suggestions can all be used by the interviewer to compare something as abstract as what to do in a difficult situation with something much more concrete, recognizable, and understandable. This process impresses on the interviewee's mind the idea that the circumstances (and solutions) in one instance can be applied to this situation as well.

The interviewer should create a collection of stories, illustrations, and suggestions corresponding to various interviewing contexts. These communication options, in conjunction with rapport, can serve as powerful, nonconfrontational aids to the interviewer endeavoring to move the subject from the "unwilling" to the "willing" chair.

For those readers interested in further exploring the concept of rapport and its uses, we recommend two excellent, foundational texts by Richard Bandler and John Grinder: *Frogs into Princes* (Moab, Utah: Real People Press) and *The Structure of Magic II* (Palo Alto: Science and Behavior Books).

Summary

The dynamics of rapport, as well as its development and its many uses, constitute the foundation of the inquiry-persuasion process. The ability to establish a rapport allows the interviewer to enter the world of the interviewee and thereby create the possibility of effecting change (behavior). Each inter-viewee is unique and provides the opportunity to learn, adjust, and develop professionally.

The strategies and techniques we have explored in this appendix might have initially seemed unfamiliar and even exotic, but on reflection, we realize:

- we have always been aware the eyes move;
- we have always known people learned through the five senses;
- people speak using sensory terms;
- people tend to reflect the mannerisms of others with whom they have a rapport;
- stories and illustrations are part of everyday communication; and
- suggestions are commonly used to influence others.

We knew these things all along; we were just not aware of the fact we knew them. Now we can perform purposefully what we once did randomly.

Appendix B

The Statement of Dr. Jeffrey MacDonald

"Let's see. Monday night my wife went to bed, and I was reading. And I went to bed about somewheres around two o'clock. I really don't know; I was reading on the couch, and my little girl Kristy had gone into bed with my wife.

And I went in to go to bed, and the bed was wet. She had wet the bed on my side, so I brought her in her own room. And I don't remember if I changed her or not; gave her a bottle and went out to the couch 'cause my bed was wet. And I went to sleep on the couch.

And then the next thing I know I heard some screaming, at least my wife; but I thought I heard Kimmie, my older daughter, screaming also. And I sat up. The kitchen light was on, and I saw some people at the foot of the bed.

So, I don't know if I really said anything or I was getting ready to say something. This happened real fast. You know, when you talk about it, it sounds like it took forever; but it didn't take forever. And so, I sat up; and at first I thought it was—I could just see three people, and I don't know if I—if I heard the girl first—or I think I saw her first. I think two of the men separated sort of at the end of my couch, and I keep all I saw was some people really.

And this guy started walking down between the coffee table and the couch, and he raised something over his head and just sort of then—sort of all together—I just got a glance of this girl with kind of a light on her face. I don't know if it was a flashlight or a candle, but it looked to me like she was holding something. And I just remember that my instinctive thought was that 'she's holding a candle. What the hell is she holding a candle for?'

But she said, before I was hit the first time, 'Kill the pigs. Acid's groovy.'

Now, that's all—that's all I think I heard before I was hit the first time, and the guy hit me in the head. So I was knocked back on the couch, and then I started struggling to get up, and I could hear it all then—now I could—maybe it's really, you know—I don't know if I was repeating to myself what she just said or if I kept hearing it, but I kept I heard, you know, 'Acid is groovy. Kill the pigs.'

And I started to struggle up; and I noticed three men now; and I think the girl was kind of behind them, either on the stairs or at the foot of the couch behind them. And the guy on my left was a colored man, and he hit me again; but at the same time, you know, I was kind of struggling. And these two men, I thought, were punching me at the time. Then I—I remember thinking to myself that—see, I work out with the boxing gloves sometimes. I was then— and I kept—'geeze, that guy throws a hell of a punch,' because he punched me in the chest, and I got this terrific pain in my chest.

And so, I was struggling, and I got hit on the shoulder or the side of the head again, and so I turned and I—and I grabbed this guy's whatever it was. I thought it was a baseball bat at the time. And I had—I was holding it. I was kind of working up it to hold onto it.

Meanwhile, both these guys were kind of hitting me, and all this time I was hearing screams. That's what I can't figure out, so—let's see, I was holding— so, I saw the—and all I got a glimpse was, was some stripes. I told you, I think, they were E6 stripes. There was one bottom rocker and it was an army jacket, and that man was a colored man, and the two men, other men, were white.

And I didn't really notice too much about them. And so I kind of struggled, and I was kind of off balance, 'cause I was still halfway on the couch and half off, and I was holding onto this. And I kept getting this pain, either in— you know, like sort of in my stomach, and he kept hitting me in the chest.

And so, then I concentrated on him. We were kind of struggling in the hallway right there at the end of the couch; and then really the next distinctive thing, I thought that—I thought that I noticed that—I saw some legs, you know, that—not covered—like I'd saw the top of some boots. And I thought that I saw knees as I was falling.

But it wasn't what was in the papers that I saw white boots. I never saw white, muddy boots. I saw—saw some knees on the top of boots, and I told, I think, the investigators, I thought they were brown, as a matter of fact.

And the next thing I remember, though was lying on the hallway—at the end of the hallway floor, and I was freezing cold and it was very quiet. And my teeth were chattering, and I went down and—to the bedroom.

And I had this—I was dizzy, you know. I wasn't really—real alert; and I— my wife was lying on the—the floor next to the bed. And there were—there was a knife in her upper chest.

So, I took that out; and I tried to give her artificial respiration but the air was coming out of her chest. So, I went and checked the kids; and—just a minute—and they were—had a lot of—there was a lot of blood around.

So, I went back into the bedroom; and I—this time I was finding it real hard to breathe, and I was dizzy. So I picked up the phone and I told this asshole operator that it was—my name was Captain MacDonald and I was at 544 Castle Drive and I needed the M.P.'s and a doctor and an ambulance. And she said, 'Is this on post or off post?'—something like that. And I started yelling at her. I said—finally, I told her it was on post, and she said, 'Well, you'll have to call the M.P.'s.'

So, I dropped the phone; and I went back and I checked my wife again; and now I was—I don't know. I assume I was hoping I hadn't seen what I had seen or I'd—or I was starting to think more like a doctor. So, I went back and I checked for pulses. You know, carotid pulses and stuff; and I—there was no pulse on my wife, and I was—I felt I was getting sick to my stomach and I was short of breath, and I was dizzy and my teeth were chattering 'cause I was cold. And so I didn't know if I was going into shock because I was so cold. That's one of the symptoms of shock; you start getting shaking chills.

So, I got down on all fours; and I was breathing for a while. Then I realized that I had talked to the operator and nothing really had happened with her. But in any case, when I went back to check my wife, I then went to check the kids. And a couple times I had to—thinking that I was going into shock and not being able to breathe.

Now I—you know, when I look back, of course, it's merely a symptom, that shortness of breath. It isn't—you weren't really that bad, but that's what happens when you get a pneumothorax. You—you think you can't breathe.

And I had to get down on my hands and knees and breathe for a while, and then I went in and checked the kids and checked their pulses and stuff. And—I don't know if it was the first time I checked them or the second time I checked them, to tell you the truth; but I had all—you know, blood on my hands and I had little cuts in here and in here, and my head hurt.

So, when I reached up to feel my head, you know, my hand was bloody. And so I—I think it was the second circuit 'cause it—by that time, I was—I was thinking better, I thought. And I went into that—I went into the bathroom right there and looked in the mirror and didn't—nothing looked wrong. I mean there wasn't really even a cut or anything. So, I—then I went out in the hall. I couldn't breathe, so I was on my hands and knees in the hall, and I—and it kept hitting me that really nothing had been solved when I called the operator.

And so I went in and—this was in the—you know, in the middle of the hallway there. And I went the other way. I went into the kitchen, picked up that phone and the operator was on the line. My other phone had never been hung up.

And she was still on the line, and she said, 'Is this Captain MacDonald?' I said, 'Yes, it is,' and she said, 'Just a minute.' And there was some dial tones and stuff and then the sergeant came on. And he said, 'Can I help you?' so, I told him that I needed a doctor and an ambulance and that some people had been stabbed, and that I thought I was going to die.

And he said, 'They'll be right there.' So, I left the phone; and I remember going back to look again. And the next thing I knew, an M.P. was giving me mouth-to-mouth respiration next to—next to my wife.

Now, I remember I saw—I don't know if it was the first or second trip into the bedroom to see my wife—but I saw that the back door was open; but that's immaterial, I guess.

That's it."

Appendix C

The Statement of O.J. Simpson

O.J. Simpson's Excerpted Statement to the Los Angeles Police Department (LAPD). This interrogation was conducted by Philip Vannatter and Thomas Lange, the Los Angeles Police Department's chief investigators of the murders of Nicole Simpson and Ron Goldman.

Vannatter: ... my partner, Detective Lange, and we're in an interview room in Parker Center. The date is June 13th, 1994, and the time is 13:35 hours. And we're here with O. J. Simpson. Is that Orenthal James Simpson?

Simpson: Orenthal James Simpson.

Vannatter: And what is your birthdate, Mr. Simpson?

Simpson: July 9th, 1947.

Vannatter: Okay. Prior to us talking to you, as we agreed with your attorney, I'm going to give you your constitutional rights. And I would like you to listen carefully. If you don't understand anything, tell me, Okay?

Simpson: All right

Vannatter: Okay. Mr. Simpson, you have the right to remain silent. If you give up the right to remain silent, anything you say can and will be used against you in a court of law. You have the right to speak to an attorney and to have an attorney present during the questioning. If you so desire and cannot afford one, an attorney will be appointed for you without charge before questioning. Do you understand your rights?

Simpson: Yes, I do.

Vannatter: Are there any questions about that?

Simpson: [unintelligible]

Vannatter: Okay, you've got to speak up louder than that ...

Simpson: Okay, no.

Vannatter: Okay, do you wish to give up your right to remain silent and talk to us?

Simpson: Ah, yes.

Vannatter:	Okay, and you give up your right to have an attorney present while we talk?
Simpson:	Mmm hmm. Yes.
Vannatter:	Okay. All right, what we're gonna do is, we want to ... We're investigating, obviously, the death of your ex-wife and another man.
Lange:	Someone told us that.
Vannatter:	Yeah, and we're going to need to talk to you about that. Are you divorced from her now?
Simpson:	Yes.
Vannatter:	How long have you been divorced?
Simpson:	Officially? Probably close to two years, but we've been apart for a little over two years.
Vannatter:	Have you?
Simpson:	Yeah.
Vannatter:	What was your relationship with her? What was the ...
Simpson:	Well, we tried to get back together, and it just didn't work. It wasn't working, and so we were going our separate ways.
Vannatter:	Recently you tried to get back together?
Simpson:	We tried to get back together for about a year, you know, where we started dating each other and seeing each other. She came back and wanted us to get back together, and ...
Vannatter:	Within the last year, you're talking about?
Simpson:	She came back about a year and four months ago about us trying to get back together, and we gave it a shot. We gave it a shot the better part of a year. And I think we both knew it wasn't working, and probably three weeks ago or so, we said it just wasn't working, and we went our separate ways.
Vannatter:	Okay, the two children are yours?
Simpson:	Yes.
Lange:	She have custody?
Simpson:	We have joint custody.
Lange:	Through the courts?
Simpson:	We went through the courts and everything. Everything is done. We have no problems with the kids, we do everything together, you know, with the kids.
Vannatter:	How was your separation? What that a ... ?
Simpson:	The first separation?
Vannatter:	Yeah, was there problems with that?

Simpson:	For me, it was big problems. I loved her, I didn't want us to separate.
Vannatter:	Uh huh. I understand she had made a couple of crime ... crime reports or something?
Simpson:	Ah, we have a big fight about six years ago on New Year's, you know, she made a report. I didn't make a report. And then we had an altercation about a year ago maybe. It wasn't a physical argument. I kicked her door or something.
Vannatter:	And she made a police report on those two occasions?
Simpson:	Mmm hmm. And I stayed right there until the police came, talked to them.
Lange:	Were you arrested at one time for something?
Simpson:	No. I mean, five years ago we had a big fight, six years ago. I don't know. I know I ended up doing community service.
Vannatter:	So you weren't arrested?
Simpson:	No, I was never really arrested.
Lange:	They never booked you or ...
Simpson:	No.
Vannatter:	Can I ask you, when's the last time you've slept?
Simpson:	I got a couple of hours sleep last night. I mean, you know, I slept a little on the plane, not much, and when I got to the hotel I was asleep a few hours when the phone call came.
Lange:	Did Nicole have a housemaid that lived there?
Simpson:	I believe so, yes.
Lange:	Do you know her name at all?
Simpson:	Evia, Elvia, something like that.
Vannatter:	We didn't see her there. Did she have the day off perhaps?
Simpson:	I don't know. I don't know what schedule she's on.
Lange:	Phil, what do you think? We can maybe just recount last night ...
Vannatter:	Yeah. When was the last time you saw Nicole?
Simpson:	We were leaving a dance recital. She took off and I was talking to her parents.
Vannatter:	Where was the dance recital?
Simpson:	Paul Revere High School.
Vannatter:	And was that for one of your children?
Simpson:	Yeah, for my daughter Sydney.
Vannatter:	And what time was that yesterday?

Simpson:	It ended about six-thirty, quarter to seven, something like that, you know, in the ballpark, right in that area. And they took off.
Vannatter:	They?
Simpson:	Her and her family—her mother and father, sisters, my kids, you know.
Vannatter:	And then you went your own separate way?
Simpson:	Yeah, actually she left, and then they came back and her mother got in a car with her, and the kids all piled into her sister's car, and they …
Vannatter:	Was Nicole driving?
Simpson:	Yeah.
Vannatter:	What kind of car was she driving?
Simpson:	Her black car, a Cherokee, a Jeep Cherokee.
Vannatter:	What were you driving?
Simpson:	My Rolls-Royce, my Bentley.
Vannatter:	Do you own that Ford Bronco that sits outside?
Simpson:	Hertz owns it, and Hertz lets me use it.
Vannatter:	So that's your vehicle, the one that was parked there on the street?
Simpson:	Mmm hmm.
Vannatter:	And it's actually owned by Hertz?
Simpson:	Hertz, yeah.
Vannatter:	Who's the primary driver on that? You?
Simpson:	I drive it, the housekeeper drives it, you know, it's kind of a …
Vannatter:	All-purpose type vehicle?
Simpson:	All-purpose, yeah. It's the only one that my insurance will allow me to let anyone else drive.
Vannatter:	Okay.
Lange:	When you drive it, where do you park it at home? Where it is now, it was in the street or something?
Simpson:	I always park it on the street.
Lange:	You never take it in the …
Simpson:	Oh, rarely. I mean, I'll bring it in—and switch the stuff, you know, and stuff like that. I did that yesterday, you know.
Lange:	When did you last drive it?
Simpson:	Yesterday.
Vannatter:	What time yesterday?
Simpson:	In the morning, in the afternoon.

Vannatter:	Okay, you left her, you're saying, about six-thirty or seven, or she left the recital?
Simpson:	Yeah.
Vannatter:	And you spoke with her parents?
Simpson:	Yeah, we were just sitting there talking.
Vannatter:	Okay, what time did you leave the recital?
Simpson:	Right about that time. We were all leaving. We were all leaving then. Her mother said something about me joining them for dinner, and I said no thanks.
Vannatter:	Where did you go from there, OJ?
Simpson:	Ah, home, home for a while, got my car for a while, tried to find my girlfriend for a while, came back to the house.
Vannatter:	Who was home when you got home?
Simpson:	Kato.
Vannatter:	Kato? Anybody else? Was your daughter there, Arnelle?
Simpson:	No.
Vannatter:	Isn't that her name, Arnelle?
Simpson:	Arnelle, yeah.
Vannatter:	So what time do you think you got back home, actually physically got home?
Simpson:	Seven-something.
Vannatter:	Seven-something? And then you left, and ...
Simpson:	Yeah, I'm trying to think, did I leave? You know, I'm always ... I had to run and get my daughter some flowers. I was actually doing the recital, so I rushed and got her some flowers, and I came home, and then I called Paula as I was going to her house, and Paula wasn't home.
Vannatter:	Paula is your girlfriend?
Simpson:	Girlfriend, yeah.
Vannatter:	Paula who?
Simpson:	Barbieri.
Vannatter:	Could you spell that for me?
Simpson:	B-A-R-B-I-E-R-I.
Vannatter:	Do you know an address on her?
Simpson:	No, she lives on Wilshire, but I think she's out of town.
Vannatter:	You got a phone number?
Simpson:	Yeah.
Vannatter:	So you didn't see her last night?
Simpson:	No, we'd been to a big affair the night before, and then I came back home. I was basically at home. I mean, any time

I was ... whatever time it took me to get to the recital and back, to get to the flower shop and back, I mean, that's the time I was out of the house.

Vannatter:	Were you scheduled to play golf this morning, some place?
Simpson:	In Chicago.
Vannatter:	What kind of tournament was it?
Simpson:	Ah, it was Hertz, with special clients.
Vannatter:	Oh, okay. What time did you leave last night, leave the house?
Simpson:	To go to the airport?
Vannatter:	Mmm hmm.
Simpson:	About ... the limo was supposed to be there at ten forty-five. Normally, they get there a little earlier. I was rushing around—somewhere between there and eleven.
Vannatter:	So approximately ten forty-five to eleven.
Simpson:	Eleven o'clock, yeah, somewhere in that area.
Vannatter:	And you went by limo?
Simpson:	Yeah.
Vannatter:	Who's the limo service?
Simpson:	Ah, you have to ask my office.
Lange:	Did you converse with the driver at all? Did you talk to him?
Simpson:	No, he was a new driver. Normally, I have a regular driver I drive with and converse. No, just about rushing to the airport, about how I live my life on airplanes, and hotels, that type of thing.
Lange:	What time did the plane leave?
Simpson:	Ah, eleven forty-five the flight took off.
Vannatter:	What airline was it?
Simpson:	American.
Vannatter:	American? And it was eleven forty-five to Chicago?
Simpson:	Chicago.
Lange:	So yesterday you did drive the white Bronco?
Simpson:	Mmm hmm.
Lange:	And where did you park it when you brought it home?
Simpson:	Ah, the first time probably by the mailbox. I'm trying to think, or did I bring it in the driveway? Normally, I will park it by the mailbox, sometimes ...
Lange:	On Ashford, or Ashland?
Simpson:	On Ashford, yeah.
Lange:	Where did you park yesterday for the last time, do you remember?

Simpson:	Right where it is.
Lange:	Where it is now?
Simpson:	Yeah.
Lange:	Where, on ... ?
Simpson:	Right on the street there.
Lange:	On Ashford?
Simpson:	No, on Rockingham.
Lange:	You parked it there?
Simpson:	Yes.
Lange:	About what time was that?
Simpson:	Eight-something, seven ... eight, nine o'clock, I don't know, right in that area.
Lange:	Did you take it to the recital?
Simpson:	No.
Lange:	What time was the recital?
Simpson:	Over at about six-thirty. Like I said, I came home, I got my car, I was going to see my girlfriend. I was calling her and she wasn't around.
Lange:	So you drove the ... you came home in the Rolls, and then you got in the Bronco ...
Simpson:	In the Bronco, 'cause my phone was in the Bronco. And because it's a Bronco. It's a Bronco, it's what I drive, you know. I'd rather drive it than any other car. And, you know, as I was going over there, I called her a couple of times and she wasn't there, and I left a message, and then I checked my messages, and there were no new messages. She wasn't there, and she may have to leave town. Then I came back and ended up sitting with Kato.
Lange:	Okay, what time was this again that you parked the Bronco?
Simpson:	Eight-something, maybe. He hadn't done a Jacuzzi, we had ... went and got a burger, and I'd come home and kind of leisurely got read to go. I mean, we'd done a few things ...
Lange:	You weren't in a hurry when you came back with the Bronco.
Simpson:	No.
Lange:	The reason I asked you, the cars were parked kind of at a funny angle, stuck out in the street.
Simpson:	Well, it's parked because ... I don't know if it's a funny angle or what. It's parked because when I was hustling at the end of the day to get all my stuff, and I was getting my phone and

	everything off it, when I just pulled it out of the gate there, it's like it's a tight turn.
Lange:	So you had it inside the compound, then?
Simpson:	Yeah.
Lange:	Oh, okay.
Simpson:	I brought it inside the compound to get my stuff out of it, and then I put it out, and I'd run back inside the gate before the gate closes.
Vannatter:	What's your office phone number?
Simpson:	
Vannatter:	And is that area code 310?
Simpson:	Yes.
Vannatter:	How did you get the injury on your hand?
Simpson:	I don't know. The first time, when I was in Chicago and all, but at the house I was just running around.
Vannatter:	How did you do it in Chicago?
Simpson:	I broke a glass. One of you guys had just called me, and I was in the bathroom, and I just kind of went bonkers for a little bit.
Lange:	Is that how you cut it?
Simpson:	Mmm, it was cut before, but I think I just opened it again, I'm not sure.
Lange:	Do you recall bleeding at all in your truck, in the Bronco?
Simpson:	I recall bleeding at my house and then I went to the Bronco. The last thing I did before I left, when I was rushing, was went and got my phone out of the Bronco.
Lange:	Mmm hmm. Where's the phone now?
Simpson:	In my bag.
Lange:	You have it … ?
Simpson:	In that black bag.
Lange:	You brought a bag with you here?
Simpson:	Yeah, it's …
Lange:	So do you recall bleeding at all?
Simpson:	Yeah, I mean, I knew I was bleeding, but it was no big deal. I bleed all the time. I play golf and stuff, so there's always something, nicks and stuff here and there.
Lange:	So did you do anything? When did you put the Band-Aid on it?
Simpson:	Actually, I asked the girl this morning for it.
Lange:	And she got it?

Simpson:	Yeah, 'cause last night with Kato, when I was leaving, he was saying something to me, and I was rushing to get my phone, and I put a little thing on it, and it stopped.
Vannatter:	Do you have the keys to that Bronco?
Simpson:	Yeah.
Vannatter:	Okay. We've impounded the Bronco. I don't know if you know that or not.
Simpson:	No.
Vannatter:	... take a look at it. Other than you, who's the last person to drive it?
Simpson:	Probably Gigi. When I'm out of town, I don't know who drives the car, maybe my daughter, maybe Kato.
Vannatter:	The keys are available?
Simpson:	I leave the keys there, you know, when Gigi's there because sometimes she needs it, or Gigi was off and wasn't coming back until today, and I was coming back tonight.
Vannatter:	So you don't mind if Gigi uses it, or ...
Simpson:	This is the only one I can let her use. When she doesn't have her car, 'cause sometimes her husband takes her car, I let her use the car.
Lange:	When was the last time you were at Nicole's house?
Simpson:	I don't go in, I won't go in her house. I haven't been in her house in a week, maybe five days. I go to her house a lot. I mean, I'm always dropping the kids off, picking the kids up, fooling around with the dog, you know.
Vannatter:	How does that usually work? Do you drop them at the porch, or do you go in with them?
Simpson:	No, I don't go in the house.
Vannatter:	Is there a kind of gate out front?
Simpson:	Yeah.
Vannatter:	But you never go inside the house?
Simpson:	Up until about five days, six days ago, I haven't been in the house. Once I started seeing Paula again, I kind of avoid Nicole.
Vannatter:	Is Nicole seeing anybody else that you ...
Simpson:	I have no idea. I really have absolutely no idea. I don't ask her. I don't know. Her and her girlfriends, they go out, you know, they've got some things going on right now with her girlfriends, so I'm assuming something's happening because one of the girlfriends is having a big problem with her hus-

	band because she's always saying she's with Nicole until three or four in the morning. She's not. You know, Nicole tells me she leaves her at one-thirty or two or two-thirty, and the girl doesn't get home until five, and she only lives a few blocks away.
Vannatter:	Something's going on, huh?
Lange:	Do you know where they went, the family, for dinner last night?
Simpson:	No. Well, no, I didn't ask.
Lange:	I just thought maybe there's a regular place that they go.
Simpson:	No. If I was with them, we'd go to Toscano. I mean, not Toscano, Poponi's.
Vannatter:	You haven't had any problems with her lately, have you, OJ?
Simpson:	I always have problems with her, you know? Our relationship has been a problem relationship. Probably lately for me, and I say this only because I said it to Ron yesterday at the— Ron Fishman, whose wife is Cora—at the dance recital, when he came up to me and went, "Oooh, boy, what's going on?" and everybody was beefing with everybody. And I said, "Well, I'm just glad I'm out the mix." You know, because I was like dealing with him and his problems with his wife and Nicole and evidently some new problems that a guy named Christian was having with his girl, and he was staying at Nicole's house, and something was going on, but I don't think it's pertinent to this.
Vannatter:	Did Nicole have words with you last night?
Simpson:	Pardon me?
Vannatter:	Did Nicole have words with you last night?
Simpson:	No, not at all.
Vannatter:	Did you talk to her last night?
Simpson:	To ask to speak to my daughter, to congratulate my daughter, and everything.
Vannatter:	But you didn't have a conversation with her?
Simpson:	No, no.
Vannatter:	What were you wearing last night, OJ?
Simpson:	What did I wear on the golf course yesterday? Some of these kind of pants, some of these kind of pants—I mean I changed different for whatever it was. I just had on some …
Vannatter:	Just these black pants.
Simpson:	Just these … They're called Bugle Boy.

Vannatter:	These aren't the pants?
Simpson:	No.
Vannatter:	Where are the pants that you wore?
Simpson:	They're hanging in my closet.
Vannatter:	These are washable, right? You just throw them in the laundry?
Simpson:	Yeah, I got 100 pair. They give them to me free, Bugle Boys, so I've got a bunch of them.
Vannatter:	Do you recall coming home and hanging them up, or ... ?
Simpson:	I always hang up my clothes. I mean, it's rare that I don't hang up my clothes unless I'm laying them in my bathroom for her to do something with them, but those are the only things I don't hang up. But when you play golf, you don't necessarily dirty pants.
Lange:	What kind of shoes were you wearing?
Simpson:	Tennis shoes.
Lange:	Tennis shoes? Do you know what kind?
Simpson:	Probably Reebok, that's all I wear.
Lange:	Are they at home, too?
Simpson:	Yeah.
Lange:	Was this supposed to be a short trip to Chicago, so you didn't take a whole lot?
Simpson:	Yeah, I was coming back today.
Lange:	Just overnight?
Simpson:	Yeah.
Vannatter:	That's a hectic schedule, drive back here to play golf and come back.
Simpson:	Yeah, but I do it all the time.
Vannatter:	Do you?
Simpson:	Yeah. That's what I was complaining with the driver about, you know, about my whole life is on and off airplanes.
Vannatter:	OJ, we've got sort of a problem.
Simpson:	Mmm hmm.
Vannatter:	We've got some blood on and in your car, we've got some blood at your house, and sort of a problem.
Simpson:	Well, take my blood test.
Lange:	Well, we'd like to do that. We've got, of course, the cut on your finger that you aren't real clear on. Do you recall having that cut on your finger the last time you were at Nicole's house?
Simpson:	A week ago?
Lange:	Yeah.

Simpson:	No. It was last night.
Lange:	Okay, so last night you cut it.
Vannatter:	Somewhere after the recital?
Simpson:	Somewhere when I was rushing to get out of my house.
Vannatter:	Okay, after the recital.
Simpson:	Yeah.
Vannatter:	What do you think happened? Do you have any idea?
Simpson:	I have no idea, man. You guys haven't told me anything. I have no idea. When you said to my daughter, who said something to me today, that somebody else might have been involved, I have absolutely no idea what happened. I don't know how, why, or what. But you guys haven't told me anything. Every time I ask you guys, you say you're going to tell me in a bit.
Vannatter:	Well, we don't know a lot of answers to these questions yet ourselves, OJ, okay?
Simpson:	I've got a bunch of guns, guns all over the place. You can take them, they're all there. I mean, you can see them. I keep them in my car for an incident that happened a month ago that my in-laws, my wife and everybody knows about that.
Vannatter:	What was that?
Simpson:	Going down to ... and cops down there know about it because I've told two marshals about it. At a mall, I was going down for a christening, and I had just left—and it was like three-thirty in the morning, and I'm in a lane, and also the car in front of me is going real slow, and I'm slowing down 'cause I figure he sees a cop, 'cause we were all going pretty fast. And I'm going to change lanes, but there's a car next to me, and I can't change lanes. Then that goes for a while, and I'm going to slow down and go around him but the car butts up to me, and I'm like caught between three cars. They were Oriental guys, and they were not letting me go anywhere. And finally I went on the shoulder, and I sped up, and then I held my phone up so they could see the light part of it, you know, 'cause I have tinted windows, and they kind of scattered, and I chased one of them for a while to make him think I was chasing him before I took off.
Lange:	Were you in the Bronco?
Simpson:	No.

Lange:	What were you driving?
Simpson:	My Bentley. It has tinted windows and all, so I figured they thought they had a nice little touch ...
Lange:	Did you think they were trying to rip you off?
Simpson:	Definitely, they were. And then the next thing, you know, Nicole and I went home. At four in the morning I got there to Laguna, and when we woke up, I told her about it, and told her parents about it, told everybody about it, you know? And when I saw two marshals at a mall, I walked up and told them about it.
Vannatter:	What did they do, make a report on it?
Simpson:	They didn't know nothing. I mean, they'll remember me and remember I told them.
Vannatter:	Did Nicole mention that she'd been getting any threats lately to you? Anything she was concerned about or the kids' safety?
Simpson:	To her?
Vannatter:	Yes.
Simpson:	From?
Vannatter:	From anybody.
Simpson:	No, not at all.
Vannatter:	Was she very security conscious? Did she keep that house locked up?
Simpson:	Very.
Vannatter:	The intercom didn't work apparently, right?
Simpson:	I thought it worked.
Vannatter:	Oh, okay. Does the electronic buzzer work?
Simpson:	The electronic buzzer works to let people in.
Vannatter:	Do you ever park in the rear when you go over there?
Simpson:	Most of the time.
Vannatter:	You do park in the rear.
Simpson:	Most times when I'm taking the kids there, I come right into the driveway, blow the horn, and she, or a lot of times the housekeeper, either the housekeeper opens or they'll keep a garage door open up on the top of the thing, you know, but that's when I'm dropping the kids off, and I'm not going in—times I go to the front because the kids have to hit the buzzer and stuff.
Vannatter:	Did you say before that up until about three weeks ago you guys were going out again and trying to ... ?

Simpson:	No, we'd been going out for about a year, and then the last six months we've had … it ain't been working, so we tried various things to see if we can make it work. We started trying to date, and that wasn't working, and so, you know, we just said the hell with it, you know.
Vannatter:	And that was about three weeks ago?
Simpson:	Yeah, about three weeks ago.
Vannatter:	So you were seeing her up to that point?
Simpson:	It's, it's … seeing her, yeah, I mean, yeah. It was a done deal. It just wasn't happening. I mean, I was gone. I was in San Juan doing a film, and I don't think we had sex since I've been back from San Juan, and that was like two months ago. So it's been like … for the kids we tried to do things together, you know, we didn't really date each other. Then we decided let's try to date each other. We went out one night, and it just didn't work.
Vannatter:	When you say it didn't work, what do you mean?
Simpson:	Ah, the night we went out it was fun. Then the next night we went out it was actually when I was down in Laguna, and she didn't want to go out. And I said, "Well, let's go out 'cause I came all the way down here to go out," and we kind of had a beef. And it just didn't work after that, you know? We were only trying to date to see if we could bring some romance back into our relationship. We just said, let's treat each other like boyfriend and girlfriend instead of, you know, like seventeen-year-old married people. I mean, seventeen years together, whatever that is.
Vannatter:	How long were you together?
Simpson:	Seventeen years.
Vannatter:	Seventeen years. Did you ever hit her, OJ?
Simpson:	Ah, one night we had a fight. We had a fight, and she hit me. And they never took my statement, they never wanted to hear my side, and they never wanted to hear the housekeeper's side. Nicole was drunk. She did her thing, she started tearing up my house, you know? I didn't punch her or anything, but I …
Vannatter:	… slapped her a couple of times.
Simpson:	No, no, I wrestled her, is what I did. I didn't slap her at all. I mean, Nicole's a strong girl. She's a … one of the most conditioned women. Since that period of time, she's hit me a

	few times, but I've never touched her after that, and I'm telling you, it's five, six years ago.
Vannatter:	What is her birth date?
Simpson:	May 19th.
Vannatter:	Did you get together with her on her birthday?
Simpson:	Yeah, her and I and the kids, I believe.
Vannatter:	Did you give her a gift?
Simpson:	I gave her a gift.
Vannatter:	What did you give her?
Simpson:	I gave her either a bracelet or the earrings.
Vannatter:	Did she keep them or ...
Simpson:	Oh, no, when we split she gave me both the earrings and the bracelet back. I bought her a very nice bracelet—I don't know if it was Mother's Day or her birthday—and I bought her the earrings for the other thing, and when we split—and it's a credit to her—she felt that it wasn't right that she had it, and I said good because I want them back.
Vannatter:	Was that the very day of her birthday, May 19, or was it a few days later?
Simpson:	What do you mean?
Vannatter:	You gave it to her on the 19th of May, her birthday, right, this bracelet?
Simpson:	I may have given her the earrings. No, the bracelet, May 19th. When was Mother's Day?
Vannatter:	Mother's Day was around that ...
Simpson:	No, it was probably her birthday, yes.
Vannatter:	And did she return it the same day?
Simpson:	Oh, no, she ... I'm in a funny place here on this, all right? She returned it—both of them—three weeks ago or so, because when I say I'm in a funny place on this it was because I gave it to my girlfriend and told her it was for her, and that was three weeks ago. I told her I bought it for her. You know? What am I going to do with it?
Lange:	Did Mr. Weitzman, your attorney, talk to you anything about this polygraph we brought up before? What are your thoughts on that?
Simpson:	Should I talk about my thoughts on that? I'm sure eventually I'll do it, but it's like I've got some weird thoughts now. I've had weird thoughts ... you know when you've been with a person for seventeen years, you think everything. I've got

	to understand what this thing is. If it's true blue, I don't mind doing it.
Lange:	Well, you're not compelled at all to take this thing, number one, and number two—don't know if Mr. Weitzman explained it to you—this goes to the exclusion of someone as much as the inclusion so we can eliminate people. And just to get things straight.
Simpson:	But does it work for elimination?
Lange:	Oh, yes. We use it for elimination more than anything.
Simpson:	Well, I'll talk to him about it.
Lange:	Understand, the reason we're talking to you is because you're the ex-husband.
Simpson:	I know, I'm the number one target, and now you tell me I've got blood all over the place.
Lange:	Well, there's blood at your house in the driveway, and we've got a search warrant, and we're going to go get the blood. We found some in your house. Is that your blood that's there?
Simpson:	If it's dripped, it's what I dripped running around trying to leave.
Lange:	Last night?
Simpson:	Yeah, and I wasn't aware that it was ... I was aware that I ... You know, I was trying to get out of the house. I didn't even pay any attention to it. I saw it when I was in the kitchen, and I grabbed a napkin or something, and that was it. I didn't think about it after that.
Vannatter:	That was last night after you got home from the recital, when you were rushing?
Simpson:	That was last night when I was ... I don't know what I was ... I was in the car getting my junk out of the car. I was in the house throwing hangers and stuff in my suitcase. I was doing my little crazy what I do ... I mean, I do it everywhere. Anybody who has ever picked me up says that OJ's a whirlwind, he's running, he's grabbing things, and that's what I was doing.
Vannatter:	Well, I'm going to step out and I'm going to get a photographer to come down and photograph your hand there. And then here pretty soon we're going to take you downstairs and get some blood from you. Okay? I'll be right back.
Lange:	So it was about five days ago you last saw Nicole? Was it at the house?

Simpson:	Okay, the last time I saw Nicole, physically saw Nicole ... I saw her obviously last night. The time before, I'm trying to think ... I went to Washington, DC, so I didn't see her, so I'm trying to think ... I haven't seen her since I went to Washington—what's the date today?
Lange:	Today's Monday, the 13th of June.
Simpson:	Okay, I went to Washington on maybe Wednesday. Thursday I think I was in ... Thursday I was in Connecticut, then Long Island Thursday afternoon and all of Friday. I got home Friday night, Friday afternoon. I played, you know ... Paula picked me up at the airport. I played golf Saturday, and when I came home I think my son was there. So I did something with my son. I don't think I saw Nicole at all then. And then I went to a big affair with Paula Saturday night, and I got up and played golf Sunday which pissed Paula off, and I saw Nicole at ... It was about a week before, I saw her at the ...
Lange:	Okay, the last time you saw Nicole, was that at her house?
Simpson:	I don't remember. I wasn't in her house, so it couldn't have been at her house, so it was, you know, I don't physically remember the last time I saw her. I may have seen her even jogging one day.
Lange:	Let me get this straight. You've never physically been inside the house?
Simpson:	Not in the last week.
Lange:	Ever. I mean, how long has she lived there? About six months?
Simpson:	Oh, Christ, I've slept at the house many, many, many times, you know? I've done everything at the house, you know? I'm just saying ... You're talking in the last week or so.
Lange:	Well, whatever. Six months she's lived there?
Simpson:	I don't know. Roughly. I was at her house maybe two weeks ago, ten days ago. One night her and I had a long talk, you know, about how can we make it better for the kids, and I told her we'd do things better. And, okay, I can almost say when that was. That was when I ... I don't know, it was about ten days ago. And then we ... The next day I had her have her dog do a flea bath or something with me. Oh, I'll tell you, I did see her one day. One day I went ... I don't know if this was the early part of last week, I went 'cause my

son had to go and get something, and he ran in, and she came to the gate, and the dog ran out, and her friend Faye and I went looking for the dog. That may have been a week ago, I don't know.

Lange: [To Vannatter] Got a photographer coming?
Vannatter: No, we're going to take him up there.
Lange: We're ready to terminate this at 14:07.